Building Campus Community

◆◆◆

Restorative Practices in Residential Life

by
Joshua Wachtel
and Ted Wachtel

Opening chapter by
Stacey Miller and Ted Wachtel

INTERNATIONAL INSTITUTE FOR RESTORATIVE PRACTICES
Bethlehem, Pennsylvania, USA

10 9 8 7 6 5 4 3 2 1
FIRST EDITION
Printed in Canada

INTERNATIONAL INSTITUTE FOR RESTORATIVE PRACTICES
P.O. Box 229
Bethlehem, PA 18016 USA

BOOK AND COVER DESIGN
Christopher MacDonald

Library of Congress Control Number: 2011962000
ISBN-13: 978-1-934355-14-5
ISBN-10: 1-934355-14-3

Table of Contents

Looking for the Magic

Chapter 1
Looking for the Magic

Every year during the summer orientation program this chapter's co-author, Stacey Miller, director of residential life at the University of Vermont (UVM), tells parents the unvarnished truth—that even under the best of circumstances, living in a campus residence hall is a difficult undertaking. Many parents, some being former college students, nod in agreement. She goes on to describe the residence hall as a unique environment where almost everyone is in young adulthood (except for a few student-affairs professionals), devoid of children, middle-aged adults and the elderly, and with the exception of fish, any animals. Yet new students enthusiastically embrace this artificial reality because their goal is simple. They want to escape parents, family members and any kind of adult supervision in their quest for independence and adulthood.

Those of us who have already experienced college life are painfully aware that, without the right support systems, residence hall living can be a recipe for disaster. Why? Because people who are in youthful stages of their emotional, mental and social development often behave in ways that are not socially responsible, civil or respectful—of themselves or others. To envision how easily civilization can turn to chaos when the young are left to their own devices, one only has to remember the boys who devolved into savagery in William Golding's classic novel *Lord of the Flies*.

Every year college and university residence halls open their doors to hundreds of thousands of first-year students who will occupy shared-living settings with a population density more concentrated than most urban residential buildings. With the exception of a few encounters at orientation or Facebook exchanges, most of these students do not know each other. Nor have most of them ever lived away from their families, except for a customary summer-camp excursion. More and more students entering college have never shared a bedroom with a sibling, and in some instances have never even shared a bathroom. Outside of directed social group activities or participation on a sports team, most have not had to live or work cooperatively with members of their peer group.

Some students have problems with alcohol and drug use. Others are boisterous, noisy, messy or rude. Some struggle with personal relationships, mental health issues, or hold racial and religious biases that interfere with their ability to connect with others. Others come with even more serious problems, such as a history of stealing or violence that is not disclosed, which eventually manifests itself in the close quarters of residential living.

In some ways residential hall living and the students who occupy these spaces are just a microcosm of the larger world, but with the inherent behaviors and characteristics of youth. Soon after their arrival on campus, they will face the demands and stresses of their academic programs—classes, assignments, exams and papers—and tensions and conflicts with roommates and friends. These are the circumstances that, every year, frame the fundamental challenge faced by the residential life staff at colleges and universities—how to build healthy communities quickly and effectively so that students can live together productively and harmoniously.

As a student affairs practitioner for more than 17 years, Stacey Miller spent much of her career in residential life looking for a formula, a "magic potion" that when dispensed would enable students in residential settings, at a minimum, to get along with each other. Many years ago she found half of that formula for healthy residential communities in the theoretical model known as "community standards." Developed at the University of Nevada, the community standards process allows students to create mutually agreed-upon expectations that define how their "community will engage and function on an interpersonal level." The model relies on dialogue to create and maintain standards because peer-to-peer interaction has been found to be the "single most potent source of influence on growth and development during the undergraduate years" (Astin, 1993); and the simple act of sharing feelings can influence and change peer perspectives and behaviors.

Through the community standards process, community members meet to discuss their needs and wants as they relate to residence hall living, make agreements based on these needs and wants and resolve difficulties that arise when agreements are not honored. Use of the community standards model is supposed to change the role of staff from authorities to facilitators and the role of students from recipients to creators of their own experiences. Theoretically, staff members are no longer expected to control but rather to guide the community toward individual and group responsibility and accountability (Piper, 1996).

But what sounded great in theory was difficult to implement in practice. Residential life professional staff members must train young resident advisors (RAs), who are in the inherently ambiguous position of simultaneously being both peer support and authorities in their relationships with the other students in their living area, to implement the community standards process. Often relying on an implicit understanding of how to develop community, residential life professional staff members would often tell RAs to build community, but they struggled to explicitly show them how. RAs were then left to figure out their own strategies and techniques to bring students together.

While some RAs are naturally communicative or charismatic, few are prepared to herd 50 or more diverse 18- to 22-year-olds together and run a meeting for any sustained period of time. How do RAs create an environment where boisterous, bored, distracted, impatient, posturing, nervous and occasionally "too cool for school" young adults will engage in meaningful dialogue about issues like roommate relationships, cleanliness and vandalism? Stacey Miller found the answer to that question—the second half of the formula for her long-sought-after magic potion—in restorative practices.

Although her colleague, Gail Shampnois, had for more than a year advocated restorative practices (RP) as a means for helping students engage and connect with each other, it was not until Stacey Miller actually participated in a restorative conversation facilitated by Charles Johnson, the safe schools consultant for the Vermont Department of Education, that she fundamentally "got it." In only a 15-minute RP circle, she learned more about some of her colleagues than she had in the eight years she had worked with them. The circle was simple, structured and provided equal status for all of the participants. While the facilitator took part in the conversation, he did not dominate or artificially control it. Rather, the "talking piece," as it was passed around the circle from person to person, ensured that respect was paid to each individual who was talking while holding the object. Although the circle is but one aspect of the RP framework, it is a very symbolic and powerful mechanism to help students get to know each other and begin the process of openly discussing their needs and wants, consistent with the community standards process.

The IIRP Graduate School (International Institute for Restorative Practices), in Bethlehem, Pennsylvania, is a leading provider of restorative practices education and training that fosters both proactive community-building and reactive "restorative justice" that responds to wrongdoing. To date, restorative approaches implemented at colleges and universities typically have been limited to restorative justice. Although the IIRP's Real Justice program was among the first to use restorative conferences to respond to wrongdoing in college settings (Wachtel, 1997), Ted Wachtel, co-author of this chapter and IIRP president, at a 1999 restorative justice conference in Australia called for "Restorative Justice in Everyday Life: Beyond the Formal Process." He suggested the systematic use of restorative approaches, not just as a response to wrongdoing, but "to guide the way people act in all of their dealings" (Strang & Braithwaite, 2001).

In 2010, in collaboration with the IIRP, UVM's residential life staff began using restorative practices both proactively and reactively. Pleased with the first year's results, UVM is now institutionalizing restorative practices so that each August RAs will participate in three days of IIRP-designed restorative practices training. (The IIRP has a training of trainers program that will transfer the training responsibility to UVM's own residential life staff.) The training and related books teach RAs how to begin the school year with proactive circles that foster community standards and then how to use a range of informal and formal restorative practices to respond to problems, conflicts and wrongdoing as they arise.

The initial circle of the school year is held with first-year students when they arrive. Passing a talking piece around the circle, RAs ask them to respond to questions like: "What are you hoping for in your first year here?" "What are your concerns?" "What are some of your long-term hopes and dreams?" These simple questions allow students to share as much or as little of themselves as they choose—but provide opportunities for students to become acquainted with each other and with the restorative circles that will be held periodically in their residence halls during the school year.

A few days later, when returning students join first-year students in the residence halls, RAs hold circles with questions designed to establish and support community standards: "What do you think the ideal residential community looks like?" "What kind of behaviors might interfere with achieving that ideal community?" "What can we as individuals and as a group do to overcome those obstacles to achieving an ideal community?" Those unfamiliar with circles are often surprised by how engaged college students become in addressing and solving behavioral issues and conflicts that are usually considered the domain of those in positions of authority. Yet the IIRP's experiences, even with students in the most challenging urban public schools and in its own model programs for delinquent and at-risk youth, have repeatedly demonstrated the validity of its fundamental premise regarding restorative practices—that people are happier, more cooperative and productive, and more likely to make positive changes when those in authority do things *with* them, rather than *to* them or *for* them.

UVM residential life staff use circles throughout the school year for a variety of purposes: to foster positive relationships, to raise consciousness about bias issues and to respond to conflicts and problems. The key to a successful circle is for facilitators to be clear in their own minds what the goal of each circle is going to be and then structure questions that promote that goal.

The most dramatic circles in UVM's first year of restorative practices dealt with a tragedy. A student who lived in the residence halls committed suicide. RAs immediately recognized the healing power of circles for resident students who were shocked, saddened and deeply troubled by the incident. Convening restorative circles within 24 hours after the tragedy allowed young people to express their feelings and support one another.

In response to substantial incidents of wrongdoing, UVM staff members have decided on two strategies. They use responsive circles when they do not know the identity of the wrongdoer and use formal restorative conferences when they do. When there is anonymous vandalism or bias graffiti, RAs convene a circle that allows students to express their feelings about the situation and to brainstorm ideas to prevent a reoccurrence. The culprit is often in the circle, hearing others' reactions to their actions and gaining an understanding of how they have adversely affected their peers. That understanding and perhaps the fear of being discovered often discourage further problems.

When the wrongdoer is known, the formal restorative conference has greater impact and is more complete. The conference facilitator asks a series of open-ended restorative questions that provide everyone with an opportunity to express themselves: first the offender, then those directly harmed, their supporters, and then those who are there to support the offender. Finally everyone has an opportunity to discuss what actions might help to restore the harm. After the formal conference, refreshments are served, providing an opportunity for informal conversation and social reintegration.

The most significant conference of the first year of restorative practices at UVM was held after a student, who was skateboarding in a hallway in violation of residential rules, inadvertently hit a sprinkler head. Water surged through the hallway into bedrooms. Firemen arrived and the building was evacuated. Students could not return to their rooms until 4 a.m., with ten rooms suffering such serious water damage that those residents had to sleep in other quarters. Books, clothing, laptop computers and beds were damaged or destroyed.

Although the student came forward to admit what he had done and his family's homeowners insurance reimbursed the losses, the young man was ashamed to face his peers. Students were angry and upset, as rumors further exacerbated feelings by creating distorted accounts of what had actually happened. While the authorities did not plan to impose punitive sanctions, in the past such an incident would have resulted in the young man moving to another residence hall in an effort to avoid the stigma. But since the advent of restorative practices at UVM, the residential life staff now had a healthier and more effective way to deal with the emotional aftermath, by inviting the young man to participate in a restorative conference.

The conference was scheduled for a Sunday evening, with 30 participants, including all the students whose rooms and property had been damaged. His roommate and his RA, who were there to support him, accompanied the young man. The staff that organized and facilitated the conference appropriately prepared everyone beforehand by letting them know what to expect.

The "offender" had the first opportunity to speak to his "victims" (these terms are never used to address or refer to anyone but are just used here to describe the conference process). When the other students realized that the incident was truly an accident, their anger subsided. Contrary to the rumors, the young man had done nothing deliberate. While he was not supposed to be skateboarding in the hallway, the consequence was obviously unintentional. He had no way of anticipating the damage that his inappropriate actions would cause. As the other students spoke, he had an opportunity to truly understand how he had adversely affected so many people in his residential community.

The conference facilitator reported that the conference went better than she had expected. The next day the student sent her an email saying, "I was skeptical going into the conference. However, I'm really glad that I was able to participate in this and I really understand how my actions affected my neighbors and fellow students." Satisfaction over the resolution of the incident was high because the conference resolved angry feelings, allowed the offender to be reintegrated into his community of peers and put the whole incident to rest.

Lesser problems in the residence halls are handled more informally. RAs might simply respond to loud music or late-night commotion or other violations with simple affective statements, telling students how their behavior makes them feel. Or they might be slightly more formal, asking a restorative question derived from the formal conference script, such as, "How do you think you are affecting others?" or after exploring feelings, "How can you make things right?" Or they might move to a small impromptu conference, bringing a few people together for an exchange, using the restorative questions to frame the discussion.

For many, being restorative is not a comfortable way of confronting behavior, states co-author Stacey Miller. For decades housing professionals have taught RAs to "lay down the law" and simply stop negative behavior. The RA is the "boss," the person who is in charge of the community, and is supposed to use that authority accordingly. Restorative practices is a huge paradigm shift in which staff confront behavior but also share their own feelings as part of that process. RAs are now told to make themselves vulnerable, express how the inappropriate behavior is impacting them and ask questions of residents to help them understand how their behavior is affecting others. Restorative practices puts the emphasis on sustaining good relationships because ultimately that is more effective in achieving behavior change. While RAs may, at times, still have an obligation to "document" students, writing up and reporting their violations of residence hall regulations, they have moved beyond a strictly legalistic and punitive approach by allowing people to have a voice, to explain what happened and to share how they have been affected, all of which create a more cordial and cooperative atmosphere in the residence halls.

While both UVM and the IIRP are committed to refining both the training and restorative protocols for residential life in their second year, they are delighted with the outcomes so far. One statistic dramatically highlights the success of the first year of restorative practices at the University of Vermont. Typically each year, by the time the winter break arrives, a dozen or more RAs have resigned from their positions, having found the job of being both peer and authority figure too frustrating and stressful to continue. However, since the implementation of restorative practices—having learned a set of strategies that allow them to be facilitators of community standards, rather than dictators—only one of UVM's 129 RAs resigned. Stacey Miller seems to have found her magic potion.

What Is Restorative Practices?

Chapter 2
What Is Restorative Practices?

The fundamental premise of restorative practices is that people are happier, more cooperative and productive, and more likely to make positive changes when those in authority do things *with* them, rather than *to* them or *for* them.

The field of restorative practices has significant implications for all aspects of society—from families, classrooms, schools and prisons to workplaces, associations, governments, and even whole nations—because restorative practices can develop better relationships among these organizations' constituents and help the overall organization function more effectively. For example, in schools, the use of restorative practices has been shown to reliably reduce misbehavior, bullying, violence and crime among students and improve the overall climate for learning (www.safersanerschools.org). Everyone who finds themselves in positions of authority—parents, teachers, police, government officials, employers and, in colleges and universities, resident advisors and residential life administrators—can benefit from learning about restorative practices.

At the International Institute for Restorative Practices' model programs, CSF Buxmont's schools for at-risk youth (www.csf-buxmont.org), the use of restorative practices has been shown to significantly reduce offending rates and improve youth attitudes. Throughout the world other successful restorative models are emerging, from single schools to entire cities, such as Hull, England, the world's first restorative city (www.hullcentreforrestorativepractice.co.uk).

An Emerging Social Science

The social science of restorative practices is an emerging field of study that enables people to restore and build community in an increasingly disconnected world. It offers a common thread to tie together theory, research and practice in seemingly disparate fields, such as education, counseling, criminal justice, social work and organizational management.

The restorative practices concept has its roots in restorative justice, a new way of looking at criminal justice that focuses on repairing the harm done to people and relationships rather than on punishing offenders (although restorative justice does not preclude incarceration of offenders or other sanctions). Originating in the 1970s as mediation between victims and offenders, in the 1990s restorative justice broadened to include communities of care as well, with victims' and offenders' families and friends participating in collaborative processes called "conferences" and "circles."

For the last decade the International Institute for Restorative Practices (IIRP), which grew out of the Real Justice program (see www.realjustice.org), has been developing a comprehensive framework for practice and theory that expands the restorative paradigm beyond its origins in criminal justice (McCold & Wachtel, 2003).

The aforementioned fundamental unifying hypothesis of restorative practices is disarmingly simple. The hypothesis maintains that the punitive and authoritarian *to* mode and the permissive and paternalistic *for* mode are not as effective as the restorative, participatory, engaging *with* mode. If this restorative hypothesis is valid, then it has significant implications for many disciplines.

For example, contemporary criminal justice and educational disciplinary practices rely on punishment to change behavior. As the number of prison inmates and excluded students grows unabated, the validity of that approach is very much in question. In a similar vein, social workers doing things *for* and *to* children and families have not turned back the tide of abuse and neglect.

Meanwhile, individuals and organizations in many fields are developing innovative models and methodology and doing empirical research, often unaware that they share the same fundamental hypothesis. In social work, family group conferencing or family group decision-making processes empower extended families to meet privately, without professionals in the room, to make a plan to protect children in their own families from further violence and neglect (American Humane Association, 2003). In criminal justice, restorative circles and conferences allow victims, offenders and their respective family members and friends to come together to explore how everyone has been affected by an offense and, when possible, to decide how to repair the harm and meet their own needs (McCold, 2003). In education, circles and groups provide opportunities for students to share their feelings, build relationships and solve problems, and when there is wrongdoing, to play an active role in addressing the wrong and making things right (Riestenberg, 2002).

In the criminal justice field these innovators use the term "restorative justice" (Zehr, 1990); in social work they advocate "empowerment" (Simon, 1994); in education they talk about "positive discipline" (Nelsen, 1996) or "responsive classrooms" (Charney, 1992); and in organizational leadership they use terms like "horizontal management" (Denton, 1998). All of these phrases are related to a similar perspective about people, their needs and their motivation. But in all of these fields, the implementation of this new thinking and practice grows only at a modest rate.

Restorative practices is the study of building social capital and achieving social discipline through participatory learning and decision-making. Through the advent of restorative practices, using its common perspective and vocabulary, there is now the potential to create much greater visibility for this way of thinking, to foster exchange between various fields and to accelerate the development of theory, research and practice.

Social Discipline Window

The social discipline window (Figure 1) is a simple but useful framework with broad application in many settings. It describes four basic approaches to maintaining social norms and behavioral boundaries. The four are represented as different combinations of high or low control and high or low support. The restorative domain combines both high control and high support and is characterized by doing things *with* people, rather than *to* them or *for* them.

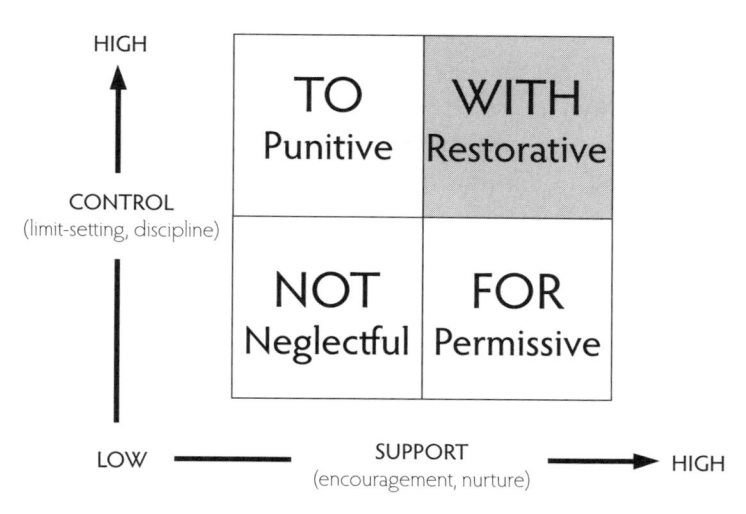

Figure 1. Social Discipline Window.

Restorative Practices Continuum

Restorative practices are not limited to formal processes, such as restorative and family group conferences or family group decision making, but range from informal to formal. Restorative practices can be used to respond to wrongdoing and conflict on a reactive basis. The restorative practices continuum (Figure 2), illustrates the range of restorative practices. The most informal restorative interactions are affective statements, which communicate people's feelings, as well as affective questions, which cause people to reflect on how their behavior has affected others. Both help build relationships by simply sharing feelings. Impromptu restorative conferences, groups and circles are somewhat more formal and structured but do not require the elaborate preparation needed for formal conferences. Moving from left to right on the continuum, as restorative processes become more formal, they involve more people, require more planning and time and are more structured and complete. Although a formal restorative process might have dramatic impact, informal practices have a powerful cumulative impact because they are part of everyday life.

Restorative practices can also be used in a proactive or preventative fashion to develop relationships, build community and reduce the likelihood or intensity of conflicts. Specifically, affective statements allow people to share their feelings in a way that creates mutual interest and bonds. Circles are especially useful as the forum for people to express their feelings safely.

Figure 2. Restorative Practices Continuum.

Affective Statements

On the informal end of the spectrum are affective statements. Sometimes these are referred to as "I statements," and they focus on someone's feelings about a given behavior: "I was sad when I heard what happened." "It warmed my heart when you came up to me the next day to offer your appreciation." "It upsets me when I hear about behavior like that on the hall." When you make these statements, you aren't necessarily looking for a reaction or immediate change, but you are trusting that being open about your feelings is good for you and that the feedback you offer may help the other person gain a bigger picture of the overall impact of their actions. Notice, too, that these statements can be positive, which is a great way to reinforce positive behavior.

Affective Questions

The word "affect" refers to the biological basis for emotion. Free expression of affect or emotion is crucial to the development of healthy relationships and communities. Affective questions—also called restorative questions—encourage people to reflect on their behavior and on their feelings.

The restorative questions asked of someone whose actions have adversely affected others are:

> ➤ What happened?
> ➤ What were you thinking at the time?
> ➤ What have you thought about since?
> ➤ Who has been affected by what you have done?
> ➤ In what way?
> ➤ What do you think you need to do to make things right?

The questions asked of those who have been harmed by others' actions are:

> ➤ What did you think when you realized what had happened?
> ➤ What impact has this incident had on you and others?
> ➤ What has been the hardest thing for you?
> ➤ What do you think needs to happen to make things right?

An RA said he found that he ended up using restorative questions a lot to follow up with residents who had been documented for some violation. "I had a pretty destructive floor this year," he added. When the bathrooms were destroyed and the next morning he found out who did it, he asked, "How do you think that makes everyone else on this floor feel when they wake up and they can't use the bathroom because there's soap everywhere in there?" It encouraged students to reflect on and change their behavior.

A campus residential life administrator explained:

Before I saw it modeled, when I first looked at the restorative questions card, the questions looked a little cheesy. Like the question, "What were you thinking?" I'd would have loved to ask that question many times, "What were you thinking when you did that!" But that's not very restorative.

But when I saw it role-modeled in our training, you were genuinely asking somebody, "What were your thoughts at the time when you were doing this? What were you thinking up to the point where you took these actions?" It's a completely different type of question than, "What were you thinking!?!" And I think it gives the person questioned an opportunity to actually talk about their perspective and where they were coming from.

When we're able to hear from people what they were thinking, it becomes, for me, much easier to see that if I were in their situation I might have actually taken the same action if I had been thinking those thoughts as well. It's allowed me to put myself in their position. Whereas in previous incidents I've sort of been stuck in my position as an administrator, and I keep them stuck in their role as a student who violated policy or who created an incident. When I'm not able to move out of those roles, I really just barrel down the road of a conduct hearing.

The restorative practices questions allow us to take some time, breathe [and say], "Let's examine this a little more slowly. Let's gather some information, see what the person was thinking, see how the community's been impacted." Once that starts to unfold, once those questions unfold, you can really see walls start to come down between people.

Anger that might have been present over incidents starts to subside a little bit. A genuine sense of care seems to emerge when people are able to hear, particularly from somebody who's violated a policy or participated in an incident, their remorse or their shame in having done something.

The restorative questions allow us to take a slower, more reflective path that's more inclusive of the community, more centered on the impact on the community. It brings in the thoughts and perspectives and feelings of the person who may have violated a policy or taken some negative actions, and it makes for a more holistic approach. It's really a community-centered approach.

The questions listed above are not the only restorative questions. Other questions will emerge naturally in response to what has happened, your relationships with the people involved, your own experience and a growing internalization of the restorative philosophy. Good RAs, good administrators, good supervisors intuitively ask these and other relationship-building questions. No one should feel that these restorative questions limit their responses, but instead should use these questions as a way to get started.

While the restorative questions above are listed in two groups, for those who have exhibited challenging behavior and those who have been affected by that behavior, in many situations there is no overt victim or perpetrator. Responsibility for a problem may be shared among a group, with everyone being perpetrators or victims in some sense, or an entire group or floor may feel that they've been victimized by some external event or action. In these cases, ask people questions like:

> What are your feelings about what has happened, and how have you been affected?

> What actions can you take responsibility for that played into this situation?

> What is your part in what happened?

> What could you do differently to help prevent such events in the future?

Other ideas for dealing with situations in which there is no clear victim or offender will be further discussed in the chapter about responsive circles.

Note that there is no "Why?" question asked, but not because you never want to discuss "Why?" In fact, it is almost always the first question people want to ask when something goes wrong. But it's a useless question. Usually no one knows why they did something wrong. And it presumes that the person asking it already knows what has happened, and now they want an explanation. Rather, it is almost always more useful and productive to first ask what happened, then what impact it had and what can be done to repair the harm and to avoid a repeat occurrence.

When the first question you ask someone involves why they did something, most of the time their defenses come up immediately. They may make up an answer they think you want to hear. Usually they'll simply look down and say, "I don't know." The fact is that when someone has done something that hurts other people or breaks a rule, they may not have had a good reason. Thoughtlessness and foolishness are usually the cause. Most people aren't able to admit that, especially if they're still trying to understand just what happened themselves. By directing the conversation to the actual event, the consequences of the actions and to what they might have done differently, it is usually easier to engage all parties. However, when victims and offenders speak directly with one another in circles and conferences, often the victim will pose the "Why?" question That is, of course, their right to ask, but as facilitators we do not ask it because it's not helpful or effective.

Small Impromptu Conferences

In the middle of the restorative continuum is the small impromptu conference. A small impromptu conference may be conducted virtually anywhere. If an RA encounters a conflict while making their rounds of the residence hall, he or she can simply ask the people involved, "What's happening?"— be it in the hall, a resident's room or in a common area. Follow-up questions will be obvious from the context of the conversation. This type of interaction generally takes no more than five or ten minutes and requires no planning other than familiarity with restorative approaches.

On a residence hall floor, a young man who was sleepwalking unintentionally entered a number of women's rooms one night.

During a small impromptu conference the next morning the young man explained that he was sleepwalking and couldn't find his way back to his room from the bathroom. The women explained that they were frightened and feared that they might be sexually assaulted. When everyone realized that what had happened was an honest mistake due to the disorientation of the sleepwalker, everyone's feelings and misunderstandings were addressed and people felt safe again.

The restorative questions are at the core of the small impromptu conference, which can be facilitated by an RA or a supervisor. The idea is to quickly resolve a minor incident or conflict. When people air their feelings and perceptions and everyone hears each other's point of view, mutual understanding generally leads to reduced tensions and resolution.

Circles

As you move from informal to formal restorative responses, the processes tend to require more time and planning. A formal circle requires forethought in terms of who will be invited to participate, what the focus will be and what questions will be asked. Proactive community-building circles for a residence floor may include "get-to-know-you" prompts and questions like, "What are your hobbies and interests?" or, "Discuss your major and why you chose it." A broad subject might also be raised such as, "What are the important issues we need to deal with on this floor?"

A resident in a suite of eight students frequently came back to the suite drunk. Her behavior was having an impact not only on herself but also on other members of the suite. Although she was not overtly violating university regulations, because she was legally of age and not drinking on the university campus, the RA for the living area approached the issue by holding a circle for all the members of the suite to discuss the general question of how things had been going in the living quarters. The suitemates discussed their expectations for the living arrangement and what people could do so that everyone would feel comfortable living together. Everybody was very open about expressing their needs and willing to make compromises with one another. After the circle meeting there were no further incidents of the resident's behavior being disruptive to others in the suite.

While this circle could be seen as responsive in that it addressed existing problems, it may also be viewed as proactive because it focused on people communicating before tensions got worse. Ideally, RAs should put more emphasis on building community than putting out fires. Holding regular proactive circle meetings makes it much easier to conduct responsive circles, and the responsive circles will be more effective.

Formal Restorative Conferences

Finally, on the far right of the continuum is the formal restorative conference. Normally, conferences are organized and conducted by someone who has been trained to run the formal process. In the IIRP's "Real Justice conference" model, there are a number of criteria that must be fulfilled before the conference takes place. The offender must have admitted to the wrongdoing and have an attitude about the conference that seems to preclude the possibility of re-victimization. The victim must also be voluntarily disposed to the conference meeting. Friends, family, affected community and other supporters of the parties will be invited to the meeting, and the process must be explained to all involved to avoid confusion during the conference. Refreshments are prepared for an informal reception after the conference, an important part of the reintegration process where people can socialize after the formal process.

A formal conference may be held for a wide variety of situations on campuses but is usually reserved for relatively serious incidents, such as theft or violence. In the case when the student flooded a building by inadvertently damaging the sprinkler head by hitting it while riding his skateboard in the hallway, the behavior itself was only a minor violation of rules and the damage caused was unintentional. But the impact was so extensive that it warranted a formal response. Conferences may also be run in parallel with disciplinary procedures. While authorities may feel that a formal punishment or sanction is

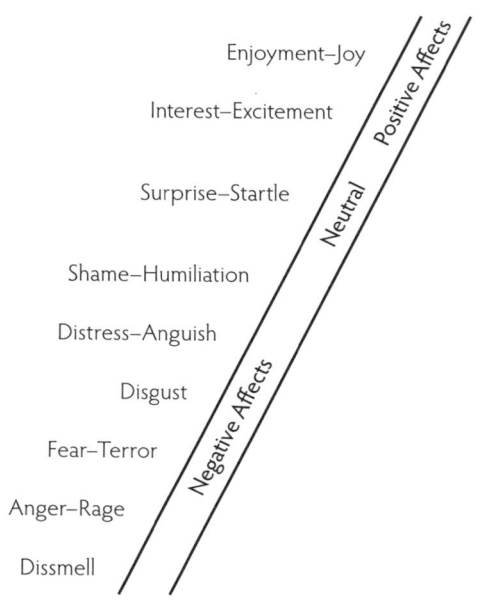

Figure 3. The Nine Innate Affects.

necessary, it is equally important to give people a chance to deal with their feelings and the damage to individuals and the community.

Tomkins' Psychology of Affect

The most critical function of restorative practices is restoring and building relationships. Because informal and formal restorative processes foster the expression of affect or emotion, they also foster emotional bonds. The late Silvan S. Tomkins' writings about the psychology of affect (Tomkins, 1962, 1963, 1991) assert that human relationships are best and healthiest when there is free expression of affect—or emotion—minimizing the negative, maximizing the positive, but allowing for free expression. Donald Nathanson, director of the Silvan S. Tomkins Institute, adds that it is through the mutual exchange of expressed affect that we build community, creating the emotional bonds that tie us all together (Nathanson, 1998). Restorative processes such as conferences and circles provide a safe environment for people to express and exchange intense emotion.

Tomkins identified nine distinct affects (Figure 3) to explain the expression of emotion in all human beings. Most of the affects are defined by pairs of words that represent the least and the most intense expression of a particular affect. The six negative affects include anger-rage, fear-terror, distress-anguish, disgust, dissmell (a word Tomkins coined to describe "turning up one's nose" at someone or something in a rejecting way), and shame-humiliation. Surprise-startle is the neutral affect, which functions like a reset button. The two positive affects are interest-excitement and enjoyment-joy.

Shame is worthy of special attention. Nathanson explains that shame is a critical regulator of human social behavior. Tomkins defined shame as occurring any time that our experience of the positive affects is interrupted (Tomkins, 1987). An individual does not have to do something wrong to feel shame; the individual just has to experience something that interrupts interest-excitement or enjoyment-joy (Nathanson, 1997). This understanding of shame provides a critical explanation for why victims of crime often feel a strong sense of shame, even though it is the offender who commits the "shameful" act.

Nathanson's Compass of Shame

Nathanson (1992, p. 132) has developed the Compass of Shame (Figure 4) to illustrate the various ways that human beings react when they feel shame. The four poles of the compass of shame and behaviors associated with them are:

> *Withdrawal*—isolating oneself, running and hiding
> *Attack self*—self put-down, masochism
> *Avoidance*—denial, abusing drugs, distraction through thrill seeking
> *Attack others*—turning the tables, lashing out verbally or physically, blaming others

Nathanson says that the "attack other" response to shame is responsible for the proliferation of violence in modern life. Usually people who have adequate self-esteem readily move beyond their feelings of shame. Nonetheless, we all react to shame, in varying degrees,

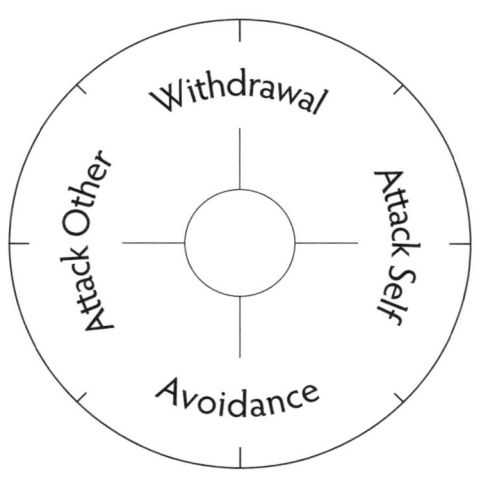

Figure 4. Compass of Shame.

in the ways described by the compass. Restorative practices, by its very nature, provides an opportunity for us to express our shame, along with other emotions, and in doing so reduce their intensity. In restorative conferences, for example, people routinely move from negative affects through the neutral affect to positive affects.

Australian criminologist John Braithwaite called this process "reintegrative shaming," which uses the natural reaction of shame in a positive way to reconnect a person to his or her community. Judicial processes and punitive measures use shame in a different way—to stigmatize offenders—but this may have the effect of driving a person to negative subcultures to find social integration, thereby working against the best interests of society.

Braithwaite argued that by "separating the deed from the doer," we can confront a person's negative behavior while at the same time affirming the goodness of the person. He noted that most people want to do right most of the time, and when people do wrong, we need to hold them accountable without increasing their shame and making them feel they no longer have a place in society. In this way, positive behavior is reinforced and the experience of shame can be used to establish new social bonds (Braithwaite, 1989).

Because the restorative concept has its roots in the field of criminal justice, we may erroneously assume that restorative practices are reactive, only to be used as a response to crime and wrongdoing. However, the free expression of emotion inherent in restorative practices not only restores but also proactively builds new relationships and social capital. Social capital is defined as the connections among individuals (Putnam, 2001) and the trust, mutual understanding, shared values and behaviors that bind us together and make cooperative action possible (Cohen & Prusak, 2001).

For example, primary schools and, more recently, some secondary schools use circles to provide students with opportunities to share their feelings, ideas and experiences in order to establish relationships and social norms on a non-crisis basis. Businesses and other organizations utilize team-building circles or groups, in which employees are afforded opportunities to get to know each other better, similar to the processes used with students. The IIRP's experience has been that classrooms and workplaces tend to be more productive when they invest in building social capital through the proactive use of restorative practices. Also, when a problem does arise, teachers and managers find that the reaction of students and employees is more positive and cooperative.

When authorities do things *with* people—whether reactively to deal with crisis or proactively in the normal course of school or business—the results are almost always better. This fundamental thesis was evident in a *Harvard Business Review* article about the concept of "fair process" in organizations (Kim & Mauborgne, 1997). The central idea of fair process is that "... individuals are most likely to trust and cooperate freely with systems—whether they themselves win or lose by those systems—when fair process is observed."

The three principles of fair process are:
> *Engagement*—involving individuals in decisions that affect them by listening to their views and genuinely taking their opinions into account
> *Explanation*—explaining the reasoning behind a decision to everyone who has been involved or who is affected by it

> *Expectation clarity*—making sure that everyone clearly understands a decision and what is expected of them in the future

Fair process applies the restorative *with* domain of the social discipline window to all kinds of organizations, in all kinds of disciplines and professions (O'Connell, 2002; Costello & O'Connell, 2002; Schnell, 2002). The fundamental hypothesis that people are happier, more cooperative and productive, and more likely to make positive changes in behavior when authorities do things *with* them, rather than *to* them or *for* them, expands the restorative paradigm far beyond its origins in restorative justice—and as explained in this book, to applications in school campus residential life.

The Resident Advisor

Chapter 3
The Resident Advisor

Recruitment is a challenge because students haven't necessarily wanted to be in a policy-enforcement role. They really are looking for student leadership opportunities. They don't want to be seen as an authoritarian and they don't want to be policing their peers.

—A Residential Life Administrator

I find this interesting correlation between the folks who have embraced the concept of restorative practices having a lot less issues in their community, and those who really haven't bought into it, who really haven't scheduled too many circles or facilitated them well, having a higher number of incidents.

—A Residential Life Administrator

Support, Control and the Role of the RA

The role of the resident advisor (RA) is complex. Most RAs sign on to do the job because they want to help build community in the residence halls, provide guidance to their resident peers and learn what it means to be in a leadership role. They want to develop relationships with residents, befriend them and help them when they need help.

While colleges and universities do support RAs in these goals, they also charge RAs with the responsibility of managing behavior, and they grant RAs a certain amount of authority to enforce campus policies, rules and regulations.

Some RAs discover this dichotomy puts them in an awkward position. One RA put it this way:

RAs play a really big double role on campus. It's a very administrative position, a person who enforces policy—and then you're a psychiatrist at the same exact time. Those are two very different things. Our job is not only to keep residents safe and build community, but it's also to enforce policy.

I'll be walking down the hall and see my residents and have a really good conversation about mountain biking or something, or they'll come and talk to me about how their girlfriend is bugging them.

But then I'll come by and be like, "Why is your closet door on your dresser with your bicycle and TV balancing on it? You can't have that. You have to put that back, otherwise you're going to get charged for that." And then they look at you like, "Weren't you the person who was just helping me with my relationship problem?" It's a very Jekyll and Hyde position that we're in.

RAs are usually 19 or 20 years old. Their residents may be a year or two younger, but they may also be the same age or older. How does one both maintain friendly relationships with peers your own age and intervene when rules have been broken? The RA quoted above went on to argue that restorative practices were helpful in that they were more consistent with a helping role.

The balance between being a peer to residents and also having authority over those peers is paralleled whenever anyone in a regular worker role suddenly finds herself promoted to a supervisory position. The difference is tangible. While you may still want to be pals with your old friends, and you probably can, there are aspects to the authority role that alter the nature of the relationship. The challenge is to manage the new role with balance, kindness and creativity.

For example, what should an RA do the first time someone comes home drunk to the hall, causing destruction and making a mess? It happens frequently on most college campuses. How can you be "restorative" when you have to confront serious misbehavior?

If it's clear that someone who has done wrong realizes and acknowledges what they've done, it is possible to use restorative questions to ask them what happened and who they think they've affected. An RA may still decide or be required to document the misbehavior, yet a positive exchange of information and emotion may also take place on the personal level.

But that will likely have to wait until later. If someone is drunk, angry, out of control or belligerent, there may be no other choice but to call campus police or draw a hard line. An RA may wonder, "Is that restorative? Can it be restorative?"

Yes, definitely. Taking a strong action in the face of danger is within the restorative framework. It is the "control" side of the social discipline window. It is restorative to make sure someone is safe and not going to hurt themselves. It can be restorative to call the police, for the safety of the person involved, others nearby and yourself. It is restorative when you follow campus regulations and protocols when faced with difficult situations.

Above all, holding a person accountable for a serious breach of conduct is most definitely restorative. Calling the police sometimes will be the most appropriate immediate response to a serious problem. But that doesn't mean you are finished in your restorative role. You may respond with restorative processes when the crisis has passed, but initially involving police may give you and the involved parties the time to reflect and decide what future actions to take.

Alternatively, if you have to write up and document an incident, while the person involved will surely not be happy about it, this action indicates to them that what they've done is serious enough to require that you bring it to the attention of campus authorities.

These types of actions may not be what people imagine restorative acts to be, but that's only if one sees "restorative" solely in terms of the "support" side of the social discipline window. Remember, however, that being restorative requires a balance of both high control and high support. Holding people accountable for their actions often means you have to take a firm stance. People are not always reasonable. When they are not reasonable, you cannot treat them the same as you would if they were being cooperative. But by definition, you are still being "restorative." It is restorative to give chances for people to change. But it is also restorative to uphold standards of behavior. It is not restorative when harsh, punitive responses are the only reaction to inappropriate behavior.

One important way to help defuse a situation is to remain calm. Of course, if a situation is serious enough that you think your best action is to call campus police, you may not feel so calm. A first-year RA during the first year of a new campus-wide restorative practices program commented, "I know how to speak restoratively in calm situations ... but in a situation that's dealing with a much more serious undertone, I didn't know how to implement restorative practices in a crisis situation."

You may try to explain to the person that when they are in a non-cooperative state, it leaves you no choice but to draw a hard line. You can tell them you would prefer not to have to write them up or call in campus authorities. By remaining emotionally reserved and to the point, you will demonstrate that you are simply doing your job. This leaves the door open for a follow-up when the person has calmed down, because they will know that this is not a personal issue for you.

What you decide to do the next day, the next week or whenever you are able to follow up on what has happened will no doubt follow along the lines of things people typically think of as "restorative." The next day you may decide to speak to the resident who came home drunk. Now that he or she is sober, it might be possible to ask restorative questions and to explain to the resident how you and others were affected by those actions. Depending on what leeway you have in terms of your authority to convene and facilitate circles, you might even ask other residents to participate in a circle so they can express how they were affected. The resident who was drunk might also ask for suggestions and support to avoid a repeat of what happened, and a plan could be made with the assistance of other residents.

If there are other administrative consequences as a result of the incident, you may still have an opportunity to explain to the resident why you did what you did and the requirements of your position and your job. And you can follow up out of genuine concern for the person's welfare. If the person continues to hold a grudge against you, you will need to make a distinction, to yourself at least, between the job you need to do and your human empathy for that person. You are not responsible for the poor choices that this person made. You just did the job you signed on to do. It may be hard for you and for them, but you can't take the other person's feelings personally.

> One of my residents was upset that I documented her for marijuana. We had a bit of an altercation. I remained calm and used restorative statements. She ended up storming out of my room and was very upset and didn't speak to me for close to a month-and-a-half. But then eventually she came to my room and apologized and thanked me for staying calm and using restorative statements. She obviously didn't use that terminology, but it kind of showed the long-term effects that using those kind of practices can have if implemented correctly, and it kind of shows that even if the effects aren't immediate, they will show up eventually.

This example illustrates the appropriate stance an RA should adopt. The RA enforced the policy about marijuana not being allowed in the residence hall while being respectful of the resident who violated the policy (and the law). Though the resident did not immediately react in a friendly way, the RA's positive intention—holding the student accountable while treating her respectfully—impacted the resident, and eventually she was able to make amends.

This is why it's so important to separate the deed from the doer—confronting behavior while affirming the inherent worth of the person.

You can't take it personally when someone blames you for upholding the rules of the college or university and doing your job. You might even sympathize with them. That doesn't mean it will always work out the way it did in the anecdote above. Even so, when you treat a person with respect, that sets a positive example, and there's always a chance that this will have a positive benefit somewhere down the line. You must know in your heart that you respect the person and that many people respond well to this type of approach.

A big part of what's being discussed here has to do with placing responsibility where it belongs—with all the members of the community. Restorative practices can help redefine the role of the RA from a policy enforcer to a key member of the community and a facilitator. For many RAs, this role feels a lot more satisfying.

An administrator commented on this, using the example of a common problem on campuses, noise:

> On some level, when the music is too loud on a floor and it's bothering other people, somebody needs to say something about it, because obviously the person who has the music on either doesn't care that it's impacting other people or doesn't really realize that it's impacting other people.
>
> In an authoritarian paradigm, people are looking for the RA to be the one to go and knock on the student's door. The reality is that we want any community member who is bothered by music to be able to knock on somebody's door and say, "Hey, you know what, it's late, I'm trying to go to bed but I can't get any sleep. You know, I can't fall asleep with the music this loud. Would you mind turning this down?"
>
> Anybody should be able to do that. When we give people the language to make those statements to interact with other community members, it really takes the RA out of that role and allows other people to share in that. Even when people feel like, "No, no, it really should be the RA this time," it still gives the RA the language to have an interaction with a resident

that doesn't have to be confrontational; it doesn't have to be acrimonious.

Sometimes when an RA comes into a situation and they're not prepared, they don't have the tools to talk to a community member, sometimes they make the interaction more hostile than it needs to be because of how they initiate the interaction. If you pound on somebody's door and say, "Hey, turn the music down," the person inside might not respond well to that, and it might start to instigate a conflict that doesn't otherwise need to have been instigated. By giving them the language to have them communicate to somebody the impact of their music, it often defuses things before they get escalated. Giving RAs that language helps them operate in a paradigm where the focus of their position is to be a community developer, rather than a policy enforcer.

Along these lines, an RA who was able to distinguish his role as a policy enforcer from that of a concerned peer made an impact with residents on the subject of alcohol use, which is illegal on many campuses, even for students who are of legal drinking age. When alcohol use and abuse became an issue on his floor, the RA held a circle. But rather than taking a hard stance from a disciplinary point of view, the RA opened up a discussion about alcohol safety. A resident reported that he thought his RA handled the situation very well. "He definitely put the emphasis on our safety rather than any disciplinary ramifications, which I thought was well played on his part," added the student.

"I've Always Kind of Been Restorative"

A frequent comment that comes up when people learn about or are trained in restorative practices is, "I've always been restorative" or, "My natural response is to be restorative." This is not surprising because a restorative practices approach is often inherent in people. However, the emerging field of restorative practices provides a practical and theoretical framework that explains a wide range of attitudes and techniques for building community and dealing with conflict. This new discipline has created an explicit vocabulary so that "restorative" can be more than intuitive—it can be discussed and learned.

When an RA says, "This isn't really much of a change from what I've always tried to do," that's all the more reason for that RA to tune into the language of restorative practices. The language gives people a terminology and an explicit framework for discussing restorative practices. Communities of RAs can share their knowledge and techniques so they can grow and reinforce their own best practices.

A public high school principal who is a strong proponent of restorative practices commented, "The reason restorative practices works is because it is based on good teaching practices. It is not some sort of convoluted system. I often find my best teachers say, 'I was doing this anyway.' Imagine if you can take what great teachers do and give other teachers a model to use it every day" (Satullo, 2011).

The same applies to residential life. There have always been great RAs and administrators who listen to their residents and those they supervise, who respect people and expect the best from them. The goal here is to share those best practices and make them more deliberate, so that residential life staff can all learn to be restorative *on purpose, all the time.*

But like any ideal, there will always be situations where, after the fact, you will say to yourself, "Wow, I wish I'd used an affective statement instead of just telling that person to stop what they were doing." Or you will wonder whether you might have organized a circle to deal with an incident before documenting it. Or you'll question whether a situation would have gone better if you'd only asked a certain person a certain question at a certain time. That questioning and checking your experience against the ideal—a perfection that no one has or ever will achieve—is what allows you to continue learning and improve your practice.

In large part, this is why the IIRP always encourages groups of individuals who have been trained in restorative practices to meet on a regular basis and exchange experiences. This is how people learn from one another and explore alternative possibilities. In dealing with any situation it is always great to know that you have options based on how others might have handled it.

The suggestion of an RA also seems relevant here: "I personally would like it if I had another RA on my staff that was kind of like my circle restorative practices buddy, so that there's always another person that my residents in our community can go to if they don't feel comfortable talking with me and who would support both me and my residents."

These are the types of ideas that come up when people talk about their practice. The restorative practices framework gives people a useful reference point. If you're already restorative, continue with it, by all means, and help reinforce this practice among your peers.

Proactive Community Circles

Chapter 4
Proactive Community Circles

I found restorative practices particularly effective right in the beginning of the year, when I was really establishing relationships on the floor. I think the use of restorative practices enabled me to form a positive relationship with my residents … an interpersonal relationship. It set the tone for the rest of the year. My residents were respectful of each other and used restorative practices within their own relationships.

—A Resident Advisor

I've had a really positive experience with restorative practices. I really have had almost an ideal experience with them. My circles are well attended. I hear the conversations afterwards about our topics. [The circles] don't end after everybody gets up. I have residents asking me frequently, "When's our next floor meeting?" So maybe I'm just doing something right, but they really can be effective. I know I've put a lot of time and effort and had to put some anger aside at times to use those restorative practices, but I've implemented them really effectively on my floor. Now I know it can be done, and I know how effective it can be.

—A Resident Advisor

Because of that community-building, it's made living where I do a better place.

—A Student

Forming the Community

Before the school year starts, RAs have as much as two weeks of training and orientation to prepare for the arrival of students. A part of this experience involves RAs getting to know one another and forming their own community. Introductory activities serve as models for the types of team-building, trust and community-creation activities that RAs will facilitate when students take up residency on campus.

Restorative practices training, which ideally is a component of RA orientation, deals not so much with RA duties and school policy—the content component of an RA's job—as with the emotional and human relations component of the job. Many RAs are drawn to the job by their natural affinity for people and a desire to take a leadership role on campus. Many will find that their leadership and social skills already contain a strong restorative streak.

This is a significant. As much as anything, restorative practices is an attitude, a stance and a posture. But it also provides a vocabulary for talking about effective ways of relating to people as well as techniques that can be used to proactively build community and address conflict.

One might even say that restorative practices is synonymous with building relationships. When people have personal connections, they tend to behave more respectfully with one another. They can talk through problems. They can plan and anticipate issues that may arise, establish goals and brainstorm forms of action. It is much harder to be uncaring and disrespectful toward another person when some kind of bond has already been formed. Plus, collective decision making is easiest and most effective when people know and care about one another.

So the first thing an RA can do when students arrive on campus is to be present and available. Introduce yourself to as many of your residents as possible. Find a connection. Let people know what your role is, where your room is and how they can communicate with you. And then invite them to your first community circle meeting.

Circles are one of the most powerful tools for community development. The circle, an incredibly flexible technique, provides a format for small as well as large groups to communicate on almost any conceivable issue.

At the very end of a restorative practices training for about 150 people, a huge circle was formed. In certain places two rows had to be made to accommodate everyone. A microphone was passed around, and everyone was asked to simply say one word to sum up their feelings or thoughts at the end of the training. It took 10 or 15 minutes for everyone to speak. While some voices expressed neutral or negative feelings or emotions, the overwhelming response was positive. All the comments provided useful feedback to the group and to the trainers.

Most circles are much smaller and allow for more in-depth conversation and meaningful expression of thoughts and emotions, but the example above shows that almost any size group is eligible for a circle experience, as long as it is framed appropriately.

This chapter will focus on how proactive circles can be used by RAs to develop community. Circles may be characterized as either proactive or reactive. Many people think that restorative practices are used for responding to problems, and that is one of its functions. But its proactive, front-end community-building actually helps prevent problems. Moreover, responsive restorative practices will be more effective when practitioners emphasize proactive measures. IIRP trainers often speak about the 80-20 rule, meaning that when an organization is on a restorative track, 80 percent of all restorative actions will tend to be proactive circles and other informal restorative practices, while only 20 percent will tend to be responsive. (Responsive practices will be addressed in Chapter 5.)

So starting the year with residence hall meetings conducted as proactive circles is an important step for laying the groundwork for building community connections. In these initial circles, you want to create a balance between people getting to know one another personally and residents exploring issues that are relevant to the community.

As with anything else that is implemented rigidly, if circles are not engaging and relevant to residents, they will fail. The first go-around in the first community circle might ask people to say their names and offer a piece of personal information—their major or academic areas of interest, hobbies, other interests, places they've traveled or what they did over the summer. These tidbits of information reveal something about people, get them comfortable with talking in circles without having to take a great risk and provide fodder for later conversations and connections between residents when they notice they have something in common with someone else in the circle.

For a second and third go-around with incoming freshmen, we advise that circles address two main questions:

> ➤ What are you hoping for in your first year here?
> ➤ What are your concerns?

Any new student will be able to relate to these questions. While some residents may feel vulnerable answering the questions, others will be inclined to share their personal feelings. Some people may choose to be more general than personal. Since all freshmen are in the same boat, they are likely to have a genuine discussion that will build compassion and mutual understanding. Some people will talk about academic classes, goals, expectations and their desire to explore subjects or pursue a certain path. Others may talk about social expectations or fears, making friends, participating in activities or sports and balancing extracurricular interests with academics. Some may talk about living away from home, dating or joining a fraternity. Whatever comes up, people will get a glimpse of one another as individuals.

When returning students join first-year students in the residence halls, RAs hold the first residence hall circle of the school year with questions designed to establish and support community standards. In this circle, RAs engage the entire community with three questions that explore the concept of an "ideal community":

1. What do you think the ideal residential community looks like?
2. What kind of behaviors might interfere with achieving that ideal community?
3. What can we as individuals and as a group do to overcome those obstacles to achieving an ideal community?

These questions are open-ended and get people to think about what they would like their living environment to be and how it should function. Some halls may be more concerned with socializing and use of common space. Others may want to create an environment that allows people to focus on their studies. Some may concentrate on creating a clean space and being respectful about personal boundaries. The shape of the conversation will very much depend on the needs and wants of the varied residents, and it is possible that different people will touch on all these themes as well as other concerns. If people's needs and wants seem to conflict, a follow-up circle could focus on the question of how people's disparate needs and wants can all be met and what compromises and support can be offered.

These groups may be very large, with as many as 40 to 60 people in attendance. We recommend that after the first two question go-arounds you break into smaller groups of about eight to ten students to talk about how to overcome the obstacles. This gives people more of a chance to participate. They'll be more engaged and less likely to get bored.

One person in each group should be selected as the facilitator to keep the group on track. Another should serve as a recorder to write down people's suggestions. At the end of the session each group's recorder will report back to the community as a whole.

The larger group will discuss and edit these ideas on a master list or a poster, which can later be hung on a bulletin board or wall in the hall where people can easily refer to it. This list continues to serve as a reminder of how the community came together to establish ideals and brainstormed ways to achieve those ideals. If such a list can't be completed in one meeting, the circle should be reconvened soon after to complete the task.

This list effectively serves as a floor contract in which residents have made commitments to one another. Later on, the poster can serve as a point of reference at a time when, inevitably, people breach the community standards. The items on the list may be revisited and revised, if needed. This list will help RAs take a restorative stance when confronting inappropriate behavior. They can point to the standards of behavior that the residents themselves said they wanted to abide by. In helping residents speak up and take ownership for their own community, some of the responsibility to police a floor now rests with residents. RAs will then find that they have succeeded in establishing a restorative posture for working *with* residents rather than doing things *to* them or *for* them. These circles at the very beginning of the year set the tone.

Tips for Facilitating Circles

When circles are new to residents, there may be questions about them, especially from returning students. It might be useful to mention the case of a sophomore whose college implemented restorative circles in her second year. She wondered aloud how many more people she would know around campus if circles had been implemented on her hall for her first year of school.

But there are other things you can tell residents, particularly if you've taken to heart the idea of circles yourself. Circles foster community. They build connections. They allow all voices to be heard. They provide a method for dealing with problems. Circles teach and facilitate conflict resolution and encourage diversity as well as mutual understanding. Be prepared for students to ask why they have been asked to participate in circles and rehearse some answers so that you feel comfortable then questioned.

Meetings of the entire floor are best, although such large groups are harder to manage. If large circles are too difficult at times, breaking into smaller groups is always an option. We've already discussed breaking into smaller circles and having people report back to the whole group at the end. One RA split her floor in half and ran two different circles at different times. She found the smaller circles were more effective and engaging, and she divided the floor in different ways for subsequent meetings so different students got a chance to meet and talk with one another. Another RA ran smaller circles for residents living in eight-person suites. This facilitated discussion between roommates about how they wanted to function within their self-contained living environment.

One of the crucial aspects to keep in mind when running a circle is to plan appropriately. You can't anticipate everything that will happen in a circle, so it's important to be as clear as you can from the start what the purpose of the circle is, what you hope to get out of it and what specific questions you will raise in order to elicit useful responses. Make sure that participants understand why you are doing circles. Remember that this may be new and uncomfortable for some residents. Understanding your rationale will help put them at ease.

At the same time, it is important that the residence hall administration not to be too rigid about circles. RAs need to take into account their residents' needs and differences when planning what to talk about in circle discussions and what approach to take. RAs need the authority to spontaneously tailor their own circles as the need arises. Rigidly formatted discussion questions from an administrative office that leave little room for RAs to adapt them tend to feel contrived and stilted and will fail to get good results.

A balance can be achieved between an administrative mandate that circles happen for residents and flexibility for RAs to approach circles in ways they deem appropriate. One residence director gives RAs general ideas for topics to cover in community circles but then asks them to write up their own specific circle questions. RAs and the director then bounce the questions back and forth by email to hone them in a collaborative process. Therefore, RAs are prepared for their circles with these thoroughly considered questions while at the same time having had a say in being creative and discovering their own ways to connect with residents.

When residents arrive and you begin your circle, be upbeat and positive. Any resistance you might encounter is probably from participants' fear and discomfort rather than a desire to be defiant. Also bear in mind that some people make jokes and tease as a social maneuver. Several students in one residence hall complained that an RA didn't understand that some of the comments they made during a circle discussion were simply meant to be sarcastic and that they were just trying to get a laugh. Trust that everyone who comes to a circle does want to get something positive out of the experience. Try and maintain a sense of humor yourself. If you find that you must address humor that seems out of place or disruptive, you might simply explain the tone you're looking to develop during the discussion or during a certain part of the circle. You could also use an affective statement to let everyone know how you feel. For example, you could say, "I know you're trying to be funny, and I do want this to be fun, but right now I'm frustrated because I do think that some of the issues we need to discuss are pretty serious, and I don't know how to convey that to you."

Another factor to consider when beginning a circle is the shape. Ask people to move so that everyone can see everyone else. If the space is awkward, if you're meeting on the floor of a hall for instance, do the best you can to encourage people to speak up, pay attention to one another and stay connected.

Sequential Circles

We strongly recommend RAs employ a sequential circle for most situations. Sequential means that everyone gets to speak, one after another, following a set pattern, usually moving person by person around the circle to the left or to the right. No one is allowed to interrupt the speaker. As explained below, often a "talking piece" is passed around the circle to identify the designated speaker.

For new facilitators this is the easiest and surest way to enable everyone to be heard. In bigger groups—and even many smaller ones—the sequential format is necessary to prevent a few vocal people from dominating a conversation. Quiet voices, which can be drowned out easily, are encouraged by the sequential circle. Many sensitive, thoughtful people hang back and keep their thoughts to themselves, preferring not to step on anyone's toes. They have great ideas but defer to bolder, louder people who continue volunteering to speak. When you assure everyone an opportunity to be heard, it is surprising how often the group gravitates toward ideas that might not have otherwise found expression.

During the writing of this book, a circle was conducted with RAs to learn more about how they were employing restorative practices. A non-sequential format was chosen at the beginning, but after the same three or four people out of fifteen had spoken multiple times, the format was changed to a sequential go-around. Even among RAs, who are leaders on campus, there were quiet people who hesitated to speak up until given a chance in turn. In subsequent meetings the sequential format was always chosen, which led to more information being shared more quickly and everyone being heard.

There are, of course, other types of circles, and these will be discussed later in this chapter. However, we start with the sequential format. This format has many advantages. It ensures that everyone knows exactly when their turn to speak will come, so people are free to listen to what everyone else has to say. In a freeform non-sequential circle, people are constantly thinking of what to say and when to say it. Also, they tend to respond to the last thing someone said rather than sitting with their thoughts until their turn comes around. The sequential format provides decorum, naturally tempering discussion and reducing the likelihood of argument or heated debate. People tend to make the points that are most relevant and important to them while considerately listening to others. The overall effect is that a wide variety of opinions get exchanged.

The facilitator may choose to begin, to model the type of response he or she is looking for. The facilitator may also choose a volunteer or draft someone at random to begin the discussion. In some cases a facilitator may ask a person or two before the meeting if they would be willing to speak first. This may help guarantee a positive tone and reduce any anxiety the facilitator may have (especially a new facilitator) about running the circle.

It may seem like a minor point, but it is a good idea to ask the first speaker to identify the direction the sequential circle will take—to the left or right of the first speaker—before that person begins to speak. If not, the person next to them usually reacts with surprise when they are asked to speak next, even though there was a 50-50 chance they would be the second speaker. By identifying the direction before the first speaker starts, you allow the person next to them to know they will be next and to get ready. Sorting it out before the conversation begins improves the flow of the circle from the outset.

Only one person speaks at a time, without interruption. The facilitator may interject briefly to keep the circle on track or to provide necessary information. The RA may also want to continue to remind people to speak loudly—as if they're speaking to the person farthest from them—because in any circle, but especially a large one, people need to be able to hear one another or else people will start to get restless and bored.

One thing to be prepared for when running a sequential circle is for people to say, "I don't know" or, "Can I pass?" RAs have reported that some residents say, "Ditto" to a previous comment and nothing else. You need to make sure you have prepared responses to these answers because it's really important to try and engage everyone in a discussion. These are young adults, and most likely they can think of something to contribute, especially if the discussion is crafted to be relevant to the participants. For instance, if someone says, "Ditto," stop and ask that person to explain why they agree with the last statement.

If someone asks to pass or asks for more time, you may skip that person and offer to come back to them later. Alternatively, you may decide to gently encourage them to respond. Forcing someone to speak when they are unwilling is counterproductive. On the other hand, it's not hard to set a positive tone and establish an expectation of participation, offering positive encouragement to residents who may be reluctant to speak. Reluctance usually results from fear and shyness rather than a desire to disrupt the circle process. Patiently waiting silently for a resident to speak may be all the encouragement he or she needs. If one or more people do pass on their turn, make a point of remembering to return to them before the circle is closed to give them a chance to speak. Again, you might simply say you'd really like to hear from everyone and ask a question to elicit what that person thinks about what he has heard.

Talking Pieces

> I have a lot of residents on my floor that are really quiet, but when they come to circles they open up and express the concerns that they have.
>
> —A Resident Advisor

While a talking piece is not required, most circle facilitators do find a talking piece to be useful in focusing attention on the speaker and maintaining order and decorum in a circle, large or small. The talking piece may be any item that can be passed safely around the circle from hand to hand. The IIRP uses a small squeezable earth ball as the talking piece for circles in its trainings.

One RA said she was uncomfortable at first about using a talking piece, but eventually she settled on passing around a bag of candy. Residents took a piece or two of candy after they finished speaking if they wanted to. Another RA used a rubber duck because it was small and durable, she didn't much care if anything happened to it, and her residents thought it was fun.

The talking piece may also be chosen as a symbol to represent something about the nature of the community or the topic being discussed. In a hall for student athletes a baseball or tennis ball could be used as a talking piece. One RA used a bar of soap as a talking piece during a discussion about keeping the hall clean. For another discussion he passed around a card with the agenda questions so that people wouldn't have to ask to be reminded what the questions were, something that happens surprisingly frequently during a circle go-around. For a circle about self-care and coping with stress, an RA chose a stress ball as a talking piece. She discovered students liked fumbling with the stress ball while thinking of what to say, so she continued using it during other circles.

Some RAs have opted not to use talking pieces. Residents told an RA, who used a small plastic frog as a talking piece, that passing items around felt juvenile to them, so she stopped using them. The rule is to do whatever works, to be flexible and respond to the expressed needs of participants. But if people don't maintain the protocol of speaking in sequence and honoring the speaker's turn, you may need to reinstitute the talking piece.

After the Circle

After the formal circle has been completed, many people will be inclined to hang around and continue talking informally. Often things that people say in the circle will serve as conversation starters. If people have been asked to offer a bit of personal information as a brief introduction—their major, places they've traveled, hobbies, etc.—people will relate to these comments in conversations with each other later.

As a facilitator, you will notice things about your residents and learn about them as people. Leaders will emerge, both the overt and talkative kind and the quiet, thoughtful variety. These are people you can count on for help and support at various points during the year. After the circle, continue to think about how you might engage your residents in making positive changes on the floor, making activities successful and even coping with problems that come up throughout the year. In future circles you might call on people you have identified as leaders to speak first during discussions or at key moments when you want support establishing a positive tone for the group.

In general, continue to build on all the relationships established in community meetings. One RA noted somewhat humorously that bathroom conversations became easier after she implemented circles on her floor. Other RAs noted that after community circle meetings they always got a friendly response from every resident in their hall.

You may want to check in with residents who missed a meeting to ask why they didn't make it and to fill them in on what was discussed. You could also ask at the end of the circle if anyone in the group would be willing to report back to those people who missed it. That way you further engage community members in the process of community building.

On Attendance, Relevance and Working with What You've Got

While college and university students are required to abide by campus policies and are accountable to their professors for their academic work, when it comes to residence hall activities there will always be residents who can take them or leave them. That can be a letdown for RAs who are genuinely committed to building community in residence halls. It's frustrating when you develop activities you think are fun and engaging, and then residents don't show up, or else they do and then make a joke of your plans. What's the answer?

To some extent, attendance is a matter of perspective. If 25 students out of 40 attend a circle, would you call that good or bad attendance? 62.5% would be a D on a test. Is that the right measure of success? Many RAs would be thrilled to see 25 residents come to a circle meeting, especially if they only expected to see a handful.

Above all, restorative practices advocates a positive, centered attitude and stance. So relax and accept that, in some real sense, the best number of people for a circle is the number that actually do show up.

Incentives like food and drink are used by some RAs to improve attendance. Competitive tactics, like halls vying to win a prize, may drive more students to meetings. One RA said she lured her residents to meetings by offering to use discretionary funds to buy them a sled if a certain number came to all her meetings. Other RAs refuse to have their floors compete for prizes, preferring to let people come to meetings for their own reasons.

Some RAs knock on everyone's door and invite residents personally to come to meetings. They tell residents how the meeting will benefit them and what will be discussed, and they describe the activities they have planned. This facilitates direct communication and develops relationships. If people can't come they might tell you why not. If they tell you they have an algebra test, a chemistry lab, a rehearsal or a big psychology paper due the next day, you've just learned something about them.

Still other RAs use email to communicate and remind residents what is going on, and they put up signs in the hallway and by the elevator. The more ways to communicate information the better, especially because different people often have very different lifestyles, habits and ways of taking in information.

Two things to remember above all:

1. The more meaningful and relevant circles and other community-building activities are to people's lives, the more likely they will be to attend and keep attending.
2. Busy schedules and conflicting demands may prevent those who would otherwise attend a circle from being able to. *Don't take it personally.*

On the first point, one RA actually sent an email to her residents to find out what topic they would like to discuss for one of their final circles. Students responded that they'd like to discuss housing and class selection. In the circle, students talked about classes and professors they really enjoyed and would recommend to others.

On the second point, it's useful to view every meeting you have as an opportunity to make connections. Every positive person you can connect with on your floor or your building contributes to your social capital. Each new relationship on a floor can make a huge difference in giving you reliable support in your role as RA. The ability to connect with people and open lines of communication that you can build on later defines leadership. When you make those connections, and when the activities and circles you plan are useful and fun for residents, those who attend will tell other people on the floor about it, and the meetings will grow.

But let's say you do have only a very small number of residents show up for a circle. What can you do? The best thing may be to simply follow the plan you made for what you expected to be a larger group. Run the activity with an air of confidence and trust that it will work. Teachers and other leaders of groups are always trying new activities, and they often feel risky to them. The best assurance of success is self-assurance. You can always modify things once they get going. In general, however, people look to the group leader for cues on how they might react. If you appear confident, that will put everyone at ease.

This especially applies when you begin to ask riskier questions in circles. Set the tone by being the first one to answer your own question or look for a volunteer if people seem uneasy. Don't ever put someone on the spot who is likely to sabotage your circle and set an uncertain tone. When you model the answer with openness, or a confident volunteer does, that begins to settle people's nerves and others will tend to follow suit.

If for some reason your planned activity is better suited to a larger group, or the activity you've planned runs short or falls apart, here are some really simple go-around questions you might try instead (recognizing that this list could be pages long):

> What's good about our floor?
> What are the major problems on our floor?
> What can those of us who are here at this meeting do to make small improvements in how our floor functions?
> Who will make a commitment to talk to three people on the floor during the next week about what was discussed at this meeting?

By the way, there is an important thing that needs to be acknowledged about groups of people. Every group is different and every circle is different. Furthermore, the exact same group of people on a different day, or a different time of day, might behave differently. When you're dealing with people, count on the unexpected.

It is the most natural thing for various groups of people, including residents on a floor, to vary radically in terms of group spirit and group dynamics. Some floors will seem apathetic, others engaged. Some will be more social and others more quiet and keep to themselves. As an RA, you can't take these differences personally. In some sense you need to trust that the challenges of working with your floor are appropriate challenges for you. Your floor, whatever its particular character and whatever unique challenges it poses, offers you the chance to exercise true creative leadership.

Creative Ways to Engage Residents in Proactive Community Circles

While supervisors will most likely provide RAs with topic ideas and guidelines about how frequently to hold community circles with residents, experience shows that flexibility is really important, too. RAs who adapt circles to suit their personalities, their residents' needs and attributes, the unique circumstances of each living situation and the common space available for meetings tend to have the best success.

An RA who had been running circles for several years during youth summer programs and with campus residents before learning the term "restorative practices" helped develop a training workshop about creative ways to engage residents. When she first became an RA she oversaw an environmental cooperative on campus, a community of 24 students wholly committed to learning everything they could about ecology, the environment and how people can effect positive change. Naturally, the circles she ran revolved around these concepts. She provided articles for the group to read about a variety of relevant topics, and these became the jumping-off point for circle discussions in which people met and exchanged opinions.

For a community meeting in a hall where residents lived in eight-person suites, this RA gave each group a blank sheet of paper and some M&Ms (the old candy incentive), and asked them to use those materials to lay out a representation of the ideal way to use their suites. This method stimulated a lot of conversation among the residents, particularly in terms of how they wanted to set up and use their common spaces.

When it came time to lead a discussion about sex and intimate relationships, which seemed to make residents nervous and anxious, this RA organized games of Texas Hold 'em using condoms as gambling chips. This relaxed the students and they ended up continuing to play throughout the entire discussion, which 33 of her 40 residents attended. The RA noted, "Since I started doing more creative and hands-on projects, I've had a lot better attendance."

But RAs could also take a more bare-bones approach to community circles by cultivating lists of simple but relevant discussion starter questions such as:

> ➤ How do you think things are going in the hall so far this year?
> ➤ What's working?
> ➤ What's not working?
> ➤ What do you think are the most important issues for us to work out as a community?
> ➤ What's one thing each person could do to help people be more connected on the floor?

The possibilities are endless, and simple questions often lead to great discussions. Open questions often allow people to express what they've been thinking but haven't had a forum for talking about. "Check-ins" or "check-outs" can be really useful, too, at the beginning or end of a planned circle or other group activity. These are brief questions that may be personally relevant or relevant to the group as a whole. Prompts could include:

> ➤ How are you doing?

> Name a highlight and lowlight from the past week (or weekend, month or day).
> Talk about something you're looking forward to in the next week.
> What are you enjoying about life on the floor?

Again, these questions allow for a quick exchange and give people a chance to learn a little more about each other. They also let you take the pulse of a group before or at the end of an activity. You may identify problems and tensions to address immediately or at another time, or people you want to follow up with later.

During a weeklong residency in a doctoral degree program in which students do much of their work from home and only travel to meet with professors and fellow students a few times per year, circle check-ins were held on a daily basis during the residency. During one of the residencies, students were housed at a hotel in the community, not on a college campus. One morning three black students discussed how they felt that they were experiencing racism in the largely white community where they were staying. One of the men said he'd been working out in a gym and felt like the owner was treating him like an angry black man, which he said was ridiculous because he was an articulate, successful professional. He believed the university should recommend places for students to stay in the community where they recognized diversity. He also said the only other people with brown faces were those he saw sweeping floors and vacuuming. People in the circle didn't know what to do about the issue, but they all said they were sorry that this had happened. In this instance, the circle process was helpful in simply allowing individuals to air feelings and receive empathy and support.

If serious issues do come up, you have to decide if you want to respond immediately with follow-up questions or simply acknowledge the issue and say you want to stay on topic and address the issue later. You might decide to address the issue at the end of the meeting or give it some thought afterward. You could consult with other

RAs or supervisors to determine what to do next. Following up with individuals and running another circle on the topics that come up are both possibilities.

Another way to facilitate connections and build relationships is to ask people to make comments about one another:

> - Explain how someone else in the circle has helped you.
> - Express a positive quality about the person to your right.
> - What is one thing you appreciate about the person to your left?
> - Say one thing you appreciate about one of your roommates.

These questions ask people to acknowledge direct, positive, personal connections. Proactive circles like these verge on being trust-building activities. Some people may feel pushed to the edge of their comfort zone and feel vulnerable expressing their personal views about other people. If people trust the circle and feel at ease, questions like these help people to develop mutual respect and understanding, openness and empathy.

Again, knowing yourself is very important. One RA commented, "Whenever I talk to RAs, I discover that something that works for one person might not work for someone else. The important thing is that RAs be able to lead discussions in a way that they feel comfortable. The more comfortable they are, the better the circles. It takes a lot of time to find that rhythm, but once you find it, the circles are so much looser."

The lesson to take away is that the more comfortable you get leading circles, the better they will be. This is just one of many good reasons to emphasize proactive circles rather than responsive circles. Facilitators and participants get more comfortable the more they speak in the circle, and this benefits the community as times goes on.

It would also be useful to note one student's reaction to feeling that her RA treated everyone fairly. "At our community circles, even when my RA's closest friends are there, she talks with all of us just as much and connects with all of us equally."

Other Types of Proactive Circles

While we strongly encourage RAs to utilize sequential circles most of the time, there are other types of circles that take more skill to facilitate but that may be useful in certain circumstances.

Non-sequential circles are more freely structured than sequential circles. Conversation proceeds from one person to another in no fixed order. This type of circle allows a discussion to evolve organically and can be used effectively for problem solving, as well.

In a non-sequential circle, people only speak when they have something they want to say. How each speaker is determined is the defining feature of the non-sequential circle, which may be highly structured, loosely structured or unstructured.

Ground rules should be established at the beginning so everyone understands the format. A talking piece may be used to help keep order and is passed from one person who is finished speaking to the next person wanting to speak. People may be required to raise their hands when they want to speak or simply ask for the talking piece. The facilitator may recognize one person at a time, or the talking piece may be passed freely to each in turn. In some groups, the facilitator may decide to allow anyone to call out or chime in at an appropriate moment without being formally recognized. This is often the case during brainstorming sessions in which you try to get a rapid-fire list of ideas, and someone may be appointed to write what people say on a board or a piece of paper so the ideas can be discussed later. The non-sequential format really depends on the specific activity.

Again, the major disadvantage of the non-sequential circle is that, unlike in the sequential go-around, not everyone is guaranteed a chance to speak. Non-sequential circles require more careful facilitation to ensure that all voices have a chance to be heard and that no one person or group of people dominate. In some situations, you may trust that those who do not speak up are still benefiting from listening to the discussion. If you do want to hear from everyone, you may ask those who have not spoken to contribute, or you might ask people who have not spoken why they haven't. If there are unknown concerns, they could come to light in a moment like that.

Alternatively, you could simply conduct a concluding sequential go-around. Ask, for example, "What is one thing you learned, realized or were surprised by about this discussion?" This way everyone gets a chance to speak and put some closure to the activity. This question, by the way, is another really useful check-out question, which can be used at the end of almost any circle or activity.

Fishbowl circles are another technique that can be both useful and fun, especially for problem solving or working with large groups. For this technique, the facilitator creates two concentric circles, a smaller inner circle with six to eight chairs, and a larger circle on the outside for the rest of the people. The people in the inner circle are the only ones permitted to speak. However, an empty chair is often left on the inside circle so that people from the outside circle who have something to say may come and occupy that chair, make their point and then return to their seat in the outer circle. That way everyone in the room feels that they have an outlet for speaking if they want to.

Take as an example a discussion about gender or bias. If you have 40 people, that may be too many to have a meaningful discussion. Instead, form an inner group of six to eight people with a common background, say all men, all women, all African-American or all minorities, and allow everyone else to sit around the outer circle. Open the discussion for the inner circle, and ask people to talk about times when they felt discriminated against or made to feel uncomfortable just because of who they are.

People might do a sequential go-around to start but then move to a non-sequential open discussion format. The discussion could be fascinating for the participants as well as the observers. If time permits, you could then add an open chair to the inside circle for those on the outside to join the discussion. Or you could allow another group of people to form a new inside circle to discuss their feelings on the topic from another perspective.

This format can also be used for a technique called "restorative problem solving." Find someone on the hall who has a problem that they're struggling with and would like to explore in a group format. It's best if the problem has relevance for others, too. Say a sophomore, who is struggling to declare a major, volunteers to present his problem to the group. He would sit in the inner circle and select five or six friends or trusted people to join him there. After presenting all his thoughts, considerations and options for about five minutes (set a time limit in advance and give a warning when the time approaches), people in the inside circle may ask a clarifying question or two, although don't allow the questions if they are really giving suggestions in the form of a question (e.g., "Have you ever tried …?").

Then a 10- to 20-minute brainstorming period begins (again, set a time limit). Discussion is limited to people offering ideas for how to resolve the problem. The person who has presented the problem does not respond except to thank the people who speak. He may write down people's responses or ask someone else to be his scribe so that he can focus on looking at and listening to the people speaking. People from the outer circle may enter the inner circle to offer their suggestions.

Brainstorming was developed in the advertising industry in New York in the 1950s as a way of getting a wide variety of ideas expressed, without comment or criticism. Then a workable plan was developed from the "brainstorms." Commenting on the ideas before the process is over dampens the creative environment and discourages suggestions.

Once the time is up or if people run out of suggestions, the person who has presented the problem can collect his thoughts and look at the list of suggestions. Finally, he says one or two things that he plans to try out. The person should not explain the choice of ideas nor critique the suggestions, but simply identify the idea or two that seem most appropriate, whether they are the same as the ideas given, a hybrid or a new idea prompted by the suggestions. The brainstorming provides an opportunity to reflect on different aspects to the problem and people's ideas for how to approach it. The fishbowl structure allows a larger audience to observe and possibly contribute.

Conclusion

When you are deciding what type of circle to choose for dealing with a given circumstance, carefully weigh the benefits of deviating from the sequential format. As soon as you do, you risk turning the floor over to the louder voices and allowing quieter voices to be squelched.

Hopefully, this chapter has given you plenty of ideas for designing and facilitating proactive circles. An even greater resource, however, will be fellow RAs and other campus circle facilitators. Use circles proactively at RA meetings so people can share what has worked and not worked for them. By this method, institutions foster the sharing of experience and the continued building of relationships in their ranks.

Responsive Restorative Practices

Chapter 5
Responsive Restorative Practices

Now when we hear about something, what we generally say is, "You need to hold a circle. Did you hold a circle? Do we need to do a formal conference?" It gives us a way of managing things. There really is something to be said for managing incidents on a case-by-case situation. There's a lot of benefit to that. But there can also be a lot of ambiguity and confusion and inconsistency. Now we have a consistent format, even though each circle might unfold differently, or one might be a responsive circle, and one might be a formal conference.

Just using restorative practices as a lens to do our work has allowed us as a department to formulate a consistency as to how we respond to students that's been really very helpful. We're not creating a new solution every time a situation arises. We are picking up a format, a paradigm that has worked in multiple ways and figuring out in a particular incident: Which community has been impacted? Who is going to lead this particular circle based on who's been impacted? How large a circle is this going to be, based on the type of incident? There still are variable details, but I feel at least now we have one type of response in restorative practices.
—A Residential Life Administrator

At the outset of the year, people generally put their best foot forward, and things usually go very well for a little while. There's no guarantee of this, of course, as some people entering college may show their true colors as early as the first day or weekend, and inevitably some RAs will find themselves dealing with serious issues, like alcohol and noise violations, from the beginning. But many communities will experience a real honeymoon period for a week, a month or more.

However, no matter how things begin, at some point issues will come up. The types of problems that come up will vary for every group, of course. While there will be isolated problems that affect just one person or a few, some problems will affect not only those directly involved, but also a wider circle of community as well.

If you think of a problem as a pebble dropped in a placid pond, the impact can be felt radiating out in concentric circles. Depending on the size of the pebble, the affected community may include roommates and other small groupings of individuals, an entire floor, multiple floors within a building, a whole building or complex and sometimes even the entire campus.

When you've done the proactive work of building community and familiarizing residents with circles as outlined in the last chapter, you'll find that your responses to all types of problems will flow quite naturally from the groundwork you have built.

Storming and Norming

According to Tuckman's Group Development Model (Tuckman, 1965), any new group of people or community goes through certain distinct stages of development. When groups form, there is often a honeymoon period. This is when people get to meet and know one another, and frequently they are on their best behavior. Tuckman referred to this as the "forming" stage of a group.

But when people start to get comfortable with each other, they may begin to act out, experience tensions, vie with each other for leadership of the group and encounter conflict about a variety of issues. This is the result of people settling into day-to-day realities and testing the waters, having different approaches and assumptions about problems and what they want and encountering personal limitations and general difficulties of communication. In Tuckman's model this breaking-in period is known as "storming." It can be tempestuous, but it can also just mean that people begin to deal with real issues. Misunderstandings and conflicts are both a symptom of the group's newness and an opportunity for people to work out their problems to become a functioning group.

While many groups get stuck at the storming level because they never fully work through their conflicts, those that do manage to press on must work through the "norming" stage. In this stage people confront their differences and conflicts and establish norms of behavior that allow the group to function. Restorative practices helps get through the trouble spots by bringing communities together to confront their problems in a real way. In circles, and with other responsive restorative practices, people are presented with a crucial opportunity to express their positions on whatever problems may come up. They can express their feelings and thoughts as well as ideas for resolution. Because everyone has input, it is often easier for groups to reach agreement even when differences of opinion remain.

As some groups resolve their differences and develop useful methods for functioning, including ways to establish or re-establish community norms of behavior, and as they come up with methods for understanding and upholding the norms, they may reach the stage Tuckman referred to as "performing." While this may be seen as a goal for any group to attain, this phase is only reached by groups that can work through their problems and differences and learn to function as an effective team.

There is fifth stage of group development, "adjourning," which is understood to be the stage at which groups dissolve and the members move on to other groupings (Jensen & Tuckman, 1977). On campuses, where groups generally adjourn either at the end of a semester or the end of the school year, this may be an important point to consider. Goodbye circles will be addressed later in this chapter.

Punishment vs. Engagement

While many residential life departments today state that their mission is to build community on campus, when it actually comes time to confront problem behaviors, campuses often resort to punitive measures. This excludes and stigmatizes community members rather than bringing them together with their peers to find community solutions to what are ultimately community problems.

Restorative practices offers a model for putting the ideal of communal problem solving into practice. An associate director of residential life on a campus that began implementing proactive community circles by having all RAs on campus trained in restorative practices commented:

> In the past when incidents happened in the halls we mostly focused on the incident, then on the person, and then on correcting that behavior. We haven't really ever had a way to engage the voices of people who were impacted. ... We also haven't had a really formalized vehicle to hear from the person responsible for the action regarding what was going on for them. We've always had a system where we really plow through the incident, get to the person, punish the person, move on to the next thing.
>
> Restorative practices has allowed us to engage community members about the impact of incidents on them. This has helped communities really strengthen their bonds. Residents are able to say to each other, "I really didn't like when you did that," or, "I can't believe you goofed off and hit the sprinkler head and flooded my room." We haven't ever had a way for students to voice that, unless they see each other in the hallway or interacted in the bathroom.
>
> But students don't necessarily take those opportunities one-on-one to say what they're feeling, particularly if they perceive it as a conflict. The way the circles are structured allows residents the opportunity to feel safe and welcome to say what

they want to say, and it's received in a way that's pretty non-threatening. It gives the person who needs to hear the message an opportunity to hear it in a safe environment, but it also allows the person who has something to say, which they might find difficult to say or conflictual, to be able to say it. That has been one of the best parts about restorative practices for us.

As we explained in the earlier story of the male student who was sleepwalking and got confused when returning from the bathroom, an innocent behavior caused a lot of intense feelings for the women who feared he was an intruder. Initially people were deeply affected, but ultimately it was clear that there was no wrongdoing. Punishments would have been useless, but doing nothing would also have been insufficient. A restorative response produced a positive outcome.

In our experience, a lot of restorative stories end this way: not dramatically, but with a sense of closure. This case would probably not have been handled through formal sanctions or with a judicial proceeding, once the authorities understood the facts. However, without administrative involvement, the circle provided an opportunity for the emotions and feelings of the people affected by the incident to be expressed aloud. The director of residential life who relayed this story commented that circles gave their staff a way to respond to all kinds of problems that unsettled a community but didn't necessarily require a formal response.

"No further problems were reported" is a common refrain when someone describes how they consciously used a restorative approach to deal with a problem. Of course this is the stated goal of punitive systems of behavior management, but punishments do not reliably stop problems and often exacerbate them. Punitive responses also fail to deal with the needs of victims and don't help people who have done wrong to understand the real consequences of their behavior.

One critique of restorative justice and restorative practices is that it is a soft approach that lets people get off without consequences. This is countered by asking what is the ultimate goal of discipline: to punish someone or to reconcile the community in the aftermath of wrongdoing?

If the point is to correct behavior but punitive measures fail to do that, what good is punishment? And if another method exists that actually works to help people modify their inappropriate behavior, whether the person is made to suffer or not, wouldn't that be preferable?

As to restorative measures being "easier," many restorative practitioners argue that asking wrongdoers to face the people they have harmed is anything but easy. Importantly, it often results in a person being able to see herself in a more honest way, which facilitates personal change and growth. Often the person will have to pay for damaged property, make apologies and take other steps to mitigate the harm done and repair relationships. These consequences are often developed by the community as a whole, with input from the person who has harmed the community. Where the only damage done is to people's emotional equilibrium, talking through issues helps heal those wounds. People mature when they have the opportunity to relate to their community this way. And the result is quite frequently that "no further problems were reported."

Responding Restoratively Through the Range of Restorative Responses

While the continuum of restorative practices lists only five techniques, it is not a cookie-cutter approach. It is as much a philosophy and attitude as it is a list of concrete responses. How your floor responds to a given problem—inappropriate alcohol, marijuana and other drug use; trashed bathrooms; roommate conflicts; racial, religious and sexual bias incidents; vandalism and petty theft; noise violations; and other problems that occur day in and day out on campuses across the country—will flow naturally from the circumstances and will take into account the creativity and resourcefulness of the community and its leaders.

Depending on the situation, there are a wide range of possible responses for RAs and administrative staff to use, from restorative statements to give and model feedback, to asking restorative questions of those involved in an incident, to organizing small impromptu conferences (which some people call mediation) for dealing with small disputes, to creating circles and formal conferences for more serious incidents that affect a wider community.

Even when confronting more serious problems, including criminal behavior, circles and formal conferences can be conducted either in lieu of or in addition to formal sanctions or judicial proceedings. These issues might include intruders on a floor and burglaries, sexual harassment and assault, inappropriate use of common spaces and fires, even student injury and death. There may be legal issues that restorative practices cannot be called upon to deal with, but for enhancing people's communication about emotional and personal responses to an incident, the range of restorative practices have a role to play.

As an RA, once you've established good relationships with people on your floor, you will find you can be that much more effective when you have to step in to confront inappropriate behavior. A university resident noted:

It is good to get to know your RA. My RA stops in and he'll hang out or he'll be like, hey, you want to go grab some dinner? That way we can kind of get to know him a little bit. That way we don't feel like he's a higher person than we are, but he's just a student, too.

By developing a friendly relationship with residents, when problems come up, the dynamic will be very different than it is for an RA who takes on a chilly and remote authority role. Here an RA simply listened to what a resident had to say about a situation, and again the resident took notice. She said:

There was a very rude note left on my door, and I left it up there. It was left by someone I didn't like, long story short, so I left it up there, and it was reported as a bias incident when they did room checks. My RA was told about it and she had to talk to me. When she talked to me, she was totally open to listening to my story. She was just really nice about it, and she was easy to talk to about it. I had a very good experience with her.

In another situation involving marijuana use by residents, the relationships established between an RA and her residents made a huge difference. Instead of having to follow up herself, a follow-up conversation was initiated by the residents themselves:

This semester three of my residents were documented for marijuana twice in a week. They actually sought me out and came to me to talk about it because they were starting to get embarrassed and kind of ashamed of what they had done. They were going to be in a little bit of trouble. But they came to me, and when I talked to them, I told them how it made me feel personally and that I was disappointed with them. I didn't ask them how it affected our community, but I did mention to them that it does. The smell does not go away very easily, so it's something to consider, and I told them that I understand for them marijuana is part of their college experience, but it's something they need to be more cautious about when they're in the residence halls.

In another situation, an RA used her relationship with residents to follow up herself. She had been off duty when trouble ensued. When she heard what happened she facilitated a fruitful conversation with her residents:

A few of my residents had been documented a couple of times in a week for what had started out as noise violation but ended in not so good a way. I just kind of followed up with them, because I wasn't the one who had done the documentation. I wasn't on duty that day or night, I guess. I just gave the residents an opportunity to say how they felt, because they felt that they hadn't been heard or given a fair shot. I was like, "Well, how do you feel about this, how is it affecting you, why did this happen, what can you do to make the situation better in the future?" and it just gave them an opportunity to have their voices heard without feeling like they were being judged. I felt like I was able to engage them and not press my RA perspective on them, but rather to let them see what effect their actions and what their friends' actions had on other people in the community.

Affective statements, restorative questions, small impromptu conferences and circles, combined with a willingness to listen, go a long way toward resolving conflict. People want to know they've been heard. When people in authority do listen, responses tend to be more appropriate. When people are engaged in fixing their own problems they assume more responsibility for themselves. An RA observed, "My residents use it with each other. They do kind of latch onto it, because it does provide an easy way to kind of get to the crux of the problem."

A big part of being restorative is realizing that you neither have to be overly punitive nor always in a position to try and resolve problems *for* people. That's why a calm and interested but not overbearing or intrusive stance can be so effective. In this case, a problem arose that was not one of policy, yet it was affecting people on the floor:

> One of our residents really enjoyed coming back from the gym very sweaty and then giving people big bear hugs. These people didn't really appreciate these sweaty bear hugs, so I used restorative practices to help facilitate a conversation between the hug receivers and the hugger.

When an RA can find that balance of involvement but not get personally wrapped up in what's going on, he or she will be able to act as a *facilitator*. An RA said, "I think restorative practices are good for small things, too, even just like one roommate complaining about another roommate being really dirty and messy and gross." In a roommate conflict, the RA doesn't have to get emotionally involved, even if he or she sympathizes more with one person than another. Rather, he or she can use restorative questions to facilitate a conversation between roommates. If they can listen and hear how their behavior affects one another, their behavior is more likely to change.

But even when specific unwanted or irritating behavior doesn't change, people can still develop more useful ways to communicate and see where each other is coming from. An RA commented, "I've been able to see restorative practices work with a lot of suitemate and roommate conflicts. It allows each suitemate or roommate to see how the other one might be feeling. I think that helps give a fresh perspective, and it's been beneficial in that way."

Another important component of all this is to simply be present and available. If you shy away from conflict, it's likely to fester. If you are forthright and bring issues to light, something positive generally comes of it. For example, a resident had a crush on an RA. This created a weird dynamic, especially since the resident was acting dramatically. For instance, when the RA was in a conversation with some other residents, the resident appeared to be jealous and left in a huff. The RA decided to respond with a text message: "I noticed you were upset about something. I really do care about you and I want to know how you are feeling. I don't like seeing you upset. I'm available to listen if you wanna talk." They spoke, and it helped clear the air.

So technology, too, can play a role in terms of fostering direct communication. People frequently imagine that other people are thinking all kinds of things about them, which is as often mistaken as correct. Drop a line (however you choose), ask for a meeting and talk things through. It's simple, but it's also restorative.

A residence director at one university found it useful to respond to residents by email when banana peels and other debris were strewn all over a stairwell in a residence hall. In the email she talked about how trash left for others to clean up has an impact on janitorial staff and the community as a whole. This seemed to be a simple, effective way to address a situation before it got out of control.

On the other hand, there can be an impersonal nature to internet communication, and some care must be taken when using a format like a mass email to not come across as authoritarian and accusatory. An RA reported that a male resident decided to have all of his hair shaven off in the bathroom. But instead of cleaning it up he left his hair on the floor. The residence director for that housing complex sent an email to the whole community about how bad it was to make such a mess in the bathroom and mentioned how this affected the custodial staff. But the residents on the floor where this happened felt put on the spot and got defensive when they read the note.

"All of my residents flipped out," commented their RA. "They felt like they were getting lectured by her for some stupid mistake by a resident in the bathroom." The RA decided to hold a circle on the floor, and she said everyone was really able to talk about how they actually felt about what the men in the bathroom had done. She noted that the female residents in particular, who had nothing to do with the incident, felt a lot better after the circle meeting.

Responsive circles serve a variety of purposes. They bring together a community that has been affected by some action or situation and allow people to air their feelings. If a single individual or group of people take responsibility for the incident, a circle gives them a chance to hear how their actions affected others and gives them a forum for explaining what happened from their point of view. The community in the circle may also present them with an opportunity to make things right.

Someone set a smoke bomb off in a carpeted hallway on a co-ed housing residential floor. The carpet caught fire, triggering the fire alarms but fortunately not the sprinklers. The police were called, and they questioned students about what had happened. Some female students told the police they believed certain men on the hall might have been involved. The police questioned these men, who denied involvement and were angry with the women who accused them. They said they believed the incident should have been resolved internally without police involvement. The police left without making any arrests, but the incident left everyone on the floor with a lot of unresolved feelings.

The residential staff decided to convene a community circle for the residents. One of the strong themes that came up was that residents really liked their floor, and they didn't like the fact that someone had set off a smoke bomb there. Some people expressed their relief that the fire was minimal and hadn't set off the sprinklers, which would have caused major damage. The students who felt defensive about having been questioned by the campus police also had the chance to express how they felt. By the end of the meeting, most of the bad feelings were defused. People trusted that everyone was committed to seeing that things like that did not happen again, and they were able to move on with their lives.

A Note on Developing Guidelines for Responding to Incidents

Of course, different campuses will develop their own protocols about how a variety of situations should be handled. One campus uses circles conducted by an RA or an administrator for situations where school policy has not been broken or in instances where the perpetrator of a violation is unknown. A more formal process, such as a conference or a traditional judicial proceeding, is employed when the person who has broken a policy is known.

But others might opt for other protocols. A variety of responses could be implemented incrementally, beginning in one area of campus life or another. Whatever the case, administrative decisions and guidelines will need to be formalized or determined informally as issues arise and decisions need to be made about how they ought to be handled.

RAs will then have to use a certain amount of discretion to know when they can deal with particular problems by convening and running circles themselves or using other more informal responses, and when they need to reach out to campus administrators for guidance. Of course, some universities will continue to deal with certain issues through traditional judicial channels. In these cases, restorative approaches could be used as an additional measure. A blending of approaches could also be developed to allow for a student who agrees to attend a circle or a restorative conference—and participate to the satisfaction of the community, RAs and campus administration—to be relieved of having to go through a formal judicial process.

Being Responsive by Being Proactive

Residential life administrators were concerned that a student who had been very troublesome and frequently documented during his first year at school would repeat his behavior in the new residential hall where he would be living in his second year. They asked his RA to convene a circle meeting early in the school year with some of his new floormates. During the circle discussion the young man articulated that he tends to act out when he feels that others aren't respecting him. He later expressed this to the larger hall community.

The line between responsive and proactive is often blurry. In the last example the facilitators attacked the root of the problem rather than wait to respond to whatever problems would manifest in year two. One might even call restorative practices a "systems theory" in the sense that it presumes that people exist not merely as individuals, but within a context or a system. When the student in the example above had the chance to articulate his self-perception that he tends to respond negatively when he thinks that others do not respect him, other students heard and acknowledged his concern. Apparently, the students in the system that surrounded him adjusted to meet the problems. No further incidents were reported to the administration.

That does not mean that it was necessarily a rosy path throughout the year. Surely issues came up. But because the RA and the students on the floor had a restorative mechanism for addressing problems, those problems never rose to the level that they had in the previous year—needing administrative intervention.

This idea of being both responsive and proactive at the same time carries through to your planning of community meetings. One college tried introducing specific topics for all students to talk about during their floor meetings any given week. But many RAs found the meetings contrived and inflexible. It may be easier and more effective to "know your audience." Have ideas for circles in mind, by all means, but don't be rigid about it. If you planned to talk about alcohol in the meeting but someone says at the beginning, "I'm sick of the trash in the bathroom every weekend," don't hesitate to gauge the room and see if others are also concerned about that same issue and whether that's what they'd like to talk about instead.

When you know your residents have an interest in a topic or when issues are starting to come up, that's the time to have a circle relating to that topic, and it is sure to go over better than a topic that feels that arbitrarily chosen. An honors college focused in an early-in-the-year meeting on maintaining quiet hours and facilitating study in the halls. If a student on the hall is expelled, the floor might want to spend time expressing their feelings about a person leaving the community and how that affects the floor.

Being responsive means sensitizing your antenna to what truly concerns your residents. For example, near the beginning of the second semester of a school year, an RA observed that inappropriate alcohol use had suddenly become an issue on her floor. She decided to run a previously scheduled community circle on the topic of responsible drinking. This allowed the RA to respond to a problem and engage residents before the issue got out of hand. Another RA did a circle on the topic of respect within the community. This was in response to a weekend when there had been a lot of vandalism in the hall.

It may be useful to note here, too, that often you will have to revisit issues. Things do come up that require more than one circle on the same topic. One way to recognize or discover if more time is needed to deal with a previously addressed issue is to ask during the next circle. A status report on a given issue may be included as a check-in question during a community circle about some other topic:

> Since our last circle was about noise on the hall, I just want to check in on how things have been going since then.

> What's the status of trash in the bathrooms and halls at the end of the weekend? Does it seem that the plan is working?

> How are people feeling about the revised study hours for finals week that were decided during our last circle?

Anticipate problems, leave openings for people to let you know their concerns and when you wonder if something is going on, simply ask. If it feels like people are giggly, nervous or down, trust your hunches. Do a quick, "How are you feeling?" go-around. If something is going on, people might tell you. And if nothing is going on, at least you checked out your feeling and can move on.

Hellos and Goodbyes

Circle meetings are also a great way to deal with mid-year introductions and goodbyes. Sometimes new residents join a floor in the middle of the year or when a new semester begins. A circle can be used to introduce them to everybody else and incorporate them into the community. This could be a component of a regularly scheduled circle, or it could be an excuse to have a circle followed by an informal gathering for people to chat and to make the new resident feel welcome.

An RA who began her job mid-year—replacing another RA who quit the job—used a circle to introduce herself and get to know residents. She acknowledged that she was coming into a community that was already established. The circle made her available to begin to make connections with people.

If a student decides to leave mid-year, a circle can be used to say goodbye. Often when people leave abruptly, they get no sense of closure, and neither does the community. A goodbye circle can be used so everyone has a chance to wish the person well and even give feedback about the impact that person had on them and the community. The person leaving may also appreciate the opportunity to give feedback to the community or to specific individuals.

At the end of a semester, before breaks or at the end of a year, circles can be used to provide closure or to mark a milestone in the course of the year. One fun method for doing this is called the "vortex." It is conducted by making an inner and an outer circle with equal numbers of people. The inner circle faces the outer and people move slowly around in opposite directions. Someone calls, "Stop," and the people facing one another at that moment exchange brief pieces of feedback. This can be done one person at a time, aloud for the group, with a person designated to call, "Stop" when they find they are facing someone with whom they would like to speak, or it can be done en masse with everyone speaking at once to the person they are facing in the other circle.

A simple go-around can also be used. Questions might include:
> What did you enjoy about the floor this year?
> What will you miss?
> What are your summer (winter, spring break) plans?
> What are your plans for next year?

The last question might help people who want to stay in touch with one another, so they can find out where people in the community plan to live and what they will be doing in the coming year.

Working with Parents

These days, parents are more and more involved in the lives of their children, even when they go off to college. It is often not enough to deal directly with students. Frequently, parents intervene when they feel their children are not getting a fair shake or when they think that their voice will carry more clout with campus authorities.

RAs, but also directors and other administrators, must field calls from parents, and often a restorative approach can be most effective.

In one case, a young man was adamant that he needed to be reassigned to a different room. The residence director for the student's housing complex spent a lot of time on the issue, talking to the young man and explaining what steps he would need to take in order to be transferred to other housing.

After some time, there was no word from the young man. Instead, his father called the director angrily and insisted that his son be moved. Rather than arguing or submitting to the student's father, the director simply asked, "Did your son explain to you that he has permission to move, and that I explained the actions he needs to take to do so?" The father was quiet for a moment and then acknowledged that he must not have been getting the full story from his son.

The director who shared this story believed it qualified as "restorative" because rather than backing down and doing things *for* the boy and his father, he told the father directly where things stood and placed responsibility back on the young man to resolve the issue if that's what he really wanted to do.

Often parents simply want to understand that their child is being treated fairly. In another case, there was tension between a female student and her RA. The residence director facilitated a meeting using restorative questions with the two and resolved the issue. When the student's mother, who had called about the issue, heard from the director how the situation was handled, she was satisfied and felt comfortable that her daughter's situation was handled in a fair way.

Student Deaths

One of the most emotionally jarring and tragic events that can happen on a campus is when a student dies. No matter the cause, fellow students are often shocked, sad and left with numerous feelings to process.

Universities have policies and protocols for announcing news like a student death to the campus. Often counselors are hired or brought in from a counseling center to be available to speak with the students who feel most upset about what has happened. But campuses that have used circles for community building will naturally use circles to process student emotions in this circumstance, as well.

A student committed suicide at a university. This was two months into the first year in which community circle meetings, facilitated by RAs, had been introduced to students across campus. Because students and staff were familiar with circles, when the suicide occurred, the natural response was to hold a series of circles, first to convey information to students about what had happened and then to allow students to meet and respond to the event in a mutually supportive way. Instead of having to call an "emergency floor meeting," students already understood what a circle was and that everyone would have an opportunity to have their voices heard.

There was a huge turnout at the first circle held that night, as 250 people gathered in the student union. People received information that confirmed and clarified some of the rumors they'd been hearing, and they had a chance to express their grief and confusion about what was going on. The discussion was open for people to talk about their feelings and ask for more information, and some people began to talk about what they wanted to do next, in terms of memorializing the student, interacting with his parents and what to do with his belongings.

Over the next several nights, a series of community circles were held throughout the student's residence complex. People checked in and expressed various needs. Administrators felt the circle was a good format because there was no expectation of participation. People could show up to the meeting or not and share what they needed to share—or not share at all—without being judged. In the circle go-around, some students passed or said, "I don't know how I feel." Some said, "This has really triggered some stuff, and I need to talk to the counseling staff later." The circle allowed for different reactions, and some floor communities spent more time processing their feelings than others. But because they already had familiarity with each other from previous circle meetings, people were comfortable sharing their feelings. Although the student's suicide was a highly emotional topic, the RAs were already experienced in facilitating circle discussions, and the process did not seem unfamiliar or awkward.

Circles played an important part of the healing process. Another circle was held for each community a week later and subsequently throughout the semester, as needed, to check in with people. Follow-up circles were helpful for people who didn't know how to respond during the first circle, including those who had said, "I don't know how I'm feeling." The follow-up circles helped them get more in touch with how they felt and allowed them to share their feelings over time.

Circles were also used with RAs and for the entire residential staff. Circles gave staff in that complex an opportunity to share among themselves, and in some cases counselors from the counseling center also joined those circles. In fact, circles, while providing a known format, proved flexible enough to allow not just the campus communities but others to participate as well, without reconfiguring the whole group dynamic.

One administrator commented, "Circles helped us move through the healing process of his death more than we would have been able to without them."

Restorative Practices in Action: Some Anecdotes

A rude comment targeting a religious group was graffitied in a hall bathroom. The RA called a meeting and did a community circle about what bias incidents are and what their impact could be.

An interesting twist to this story is that the RA made a game of it. Everyone stood in a circle facing in, and the RA read off a number of statements about identity and various experiences. Anyone who felt that the statement pertained to them had to step into the center of the circle for a moment. One of the prompts was to step in if you felt affected by the graffiti.

A student commented that the exercise helped make him more aware of the people's different identities and experiences. He also said he believed that it was easier for people to speak up because they weren't put on the spot nor compelled to condemn the graffiti writer without knowing his or her intentions.

◆ ◆ ◆

A residence director (RD) overseeing a housing complex had her door vandalized, possibly by multiple people, and some of the graffiti was sexist in nature. The culprits were not known, and the RD was upset about the event and didn't feel safe.

The staff decided to hold a circle meeting and to combine two floors, one all male and the other all female. The men were invited to the lounge on the women's floor, and everyone had a chance to hear about what had happened and to talk about how they might be feeling. The women in particular appreciated the opportunity to admit during the discussion that they hadn't felt safe in the community because of such incidents. They thanked the staff for raising the issue and said afterward that they felt validated in having the opportunity to say how they felt.

The administrator who conveyed this anecdote commented, "Most folks when they do something like that think they're getting back at the residence director for upholding policy. They aren't thinking about how they might be affecting other people. Now we know we can call on the female residents who are also part of the affected community."

◆ ◆ ◆

During orientation for first-year students, an upper-class orienter was caught drinking on campus. The head of residential life called a circle for the upperclassmen and the freshmen he was orienting so they could express their feelings about what had happened.

Previously, when punitive measures were taken to confront a student about drinking, the student frequently responded by saying, "What's the big deal?" In this case, the student realized that people trusted him and was able to see how they were directly impacted by his behavior. As a result of the meeting, he felt humbled.

◆❖◆

An unknown intruder entered a room and urinated on the floor. He or she was not caught. The floor's RA helped residents clean up the mess. Afterward, they all sat down and had a small impromptu conference together to discuss how they felt about what had happened.

The next evening, the RA called a circle meeting for the whole floor. She had just begun her job, replacing an RA who had left his position mid-year. "Coming into the community straight away and having this issue," she commented, "... It was really nice to see all the residents, how they reacted and how they all were concerned about the issue."

◆❖◆

There was an ongoing issue involving excessive partying on a floor. The RA convened a meeting, left the room and let the students on the floor talk about the problems. During the meeting, the residents said that everyone realized and acknowledged that the RA had a responsibility to maintain decorum on the floor and that they didn't want to cause him extra trouble. The group talked about all the relevant issues and came up with ideas for addressing them. By the end of the session, they had made a plan that included residents speaking directly to one another when they might see someone being too loud or doing something else that isn't allowed.

This process is reminiscent of the "family group conference" or "family group decision making" process, in which the professionals frame a discussion for a family and close supporters but then leave the room and allow the participating community to discuss their problems in private and develop a plan, which is then presented to the professionals. A student who attended the circle commented, "You're not going to admit what you've done if the RA is there."

◆◆◆

An RA who was among the most resistant to using restorative practices went to her director, exasperated about a group of students that was driving her crazy. She said that no matter what she did, the inappropriate behavior persisted. Most recently, over the weekend, she had written up discipline reports on nine students who were drinking alcohol in the residence hall.

Her director said, "Let's schedule a circle meeting with all those students," and assured her that if that didn't work, they might have to ask some of the students to move out of the residence hall. The director then facilitated a circle discussion with the students and the RA.

In the circle, the director asked, "Why do you think we're having this conversation now?" The students acknowledged that it was because of the trouble they'd been causing on the hall and for having been written up for alcohol use. He then asked, "What impact do you think your behavior is having on the other residents and your RA?"

The students tried to answer this, but the biggest impact came when the RA herself spoke. She said, "I don't even want to go to the back of the hallway because I'm afraid of all of you and what I'll find going on there." The residents were shocked. They said, "We like you, and we didn't want to have this impact." Afterward they said, "We appreciate being able to have this conversation and have a word with both of you, rather than just being punished."

When the director followed up with the RA a few days later, she reported that things were better on the floor. The director reminded her that the expectation for the circle was not that it would make things perfect forever, and that the RA would eventually deal with more issues with that group of students. Nonetheless the RA, who had been known for her skeptical attitude toward restorative practices from the start, laughingly acknowledged, "Dammit, it worked again!"

Other Implications

Beyond their use in residential settings, restorative practices has great potential for colleges and universities. A growing number of institutions use restorative justice to respond to student misconduct in lieu of traditional hearings. Restorative justice provides both wrongdoers and those they have harmed with better outcomes—repairing harm and restoring relationships. Offending students have the opportunity to redeem themselves and continue their education, whereas in the past they have often been suspended or expelled. Further, victims achieve a sense of fairness and justice that is not possible when school authorities simply impose sanctions.

Restorative practices can also improve "town and gown" relations (those between local residents and college students). Engaging students with their neighbors when problems arise will achieve more satisfying and effective resolution. Most students start their undergraduate experience in college housing, providing a good opportunity to experience restorative practices. When students move to off-campus housing in later years, their previous exposure to restorative practices on campus may improve their sense of community, empathy and personal responsibility.

Finally, professors who use circles will find that they engage students more effectively, encourage quiet students to speak and enhance the overall sense of connectedness in their classrooms.

CHAPTER 6

Old as the Hills

Chapter 6
Old as the Hills

Restorative practices in school campus residential settings, from informal affective statements and questions to formal restorative conferences, is an effective and satisfying ways of developing community and responding to problems. Shifting from unproductive punitive and authoritarian strategies that fail to achieve social discipline, restorative practices also provides a hopeful model for society itself to reduce crime, violence and conflict.

Circles are of special interest because they are as old as the hills. Human beings' earliest discussions were held in circles around the fire. Somewhere along the way, as our numbers grew and our social organizations became more complex, we moved out of egalitarian circles into hierarchical structures. Now, often from a raised platform, leaders typically face their constituents who are seated in rows, with most of the group looking at the backs of the people in front of them.

Yet, in a variety of settings and for a variety of purposes, we are rediscovering the power of circles. For all our technological advances, we have come to realize that we lost something along the way—a very simple and effective technology that fosters mutual understanding and healing with outcomes that often seem magical.

In circles, we face each other and speak respectfully, one person at a time, diminishing the feeling of disconnectedness that permeates our modern world and restoring the sense of belonging that constitutes healthy human community. We may find that this ancient form of social discourse helps us address our greatest challenges (Costello, Wachtel & Wachtel, 2010).

References

American Humane Association (2003). FGDM Research and Evaluation. *Protecting Children*, 18(1-2): whole volume.

Astin, A.W. (1993). *What matters in college? Four critical years revisited.* San Francisco: Jossey-Bass.

Braithwaite, J. (1989). *Crime, Shame and Reintegration.* Cambridge, UK: Cambridge University Press.

Charney, R. (1992). *Teaching Children to Care: Management in the Responsive Classroom.* Greenfield, MA: Northeast Foundation for Children.

Cohen, D., & Prusak, L. (2001). *In Good Company: How Social Capital Makes Organizations Work.* Boston: Harvard Business School Press.

Costello, B., & O'Connell, T. (2002, August). Restorative practices in the workplace. Paper presented at the Third International Conference on Conferencing, Circles and other Restorative Practices, Minneapolis, MN.

Costello, B., Wachtel, J., & Wachtel, T. (2010). *Restorative Circles in Schools: Building Community and Enhancing Learning.* Bethlehem, PA: IIRP.

Denton, D. (1998). *Horizontal Management.* Lanham, MD: Rowman and Littlefield.

Golding, W. (1954). *Lord of the Flies,* London: Faber and Faber.

Jensen, M., & Tuckman, B. (1977, December). Stages of small-group development revisited. *Group & Organization Studies.* 2, 4; ABI/INFORM Global pg. 419.

Kim, W., & Mauborgne, R. (1997). Fair process. *Harvard Business Review,* January 1.

McCold, P. (2003). A survey of assessment research on mediation and conferencing. In L. Walgrave (Ed.), *Repositioning Restorative Justice* (pp. 67-120). Devon, UK: Willan Publishing.

McCold, P., & Wachtel, T. (2003, August). In pursuit of paradigm: A theory of restorative justice. Paper presented at the XIII World Congress of Criminology, Rio de Janeiro, Brazil. http://www. realjustice.org/library/paradigm.html

Nathanson, D.L. (1992). *Shame and Pride: Affect, Sex, and the Birth of the Self.* New York: Norton.

Nathanson, D.L. (1997). Affect theory and the compass of shame. In M. Lansky and A. Morrison (Eds.), *The Widening Scope of Shame.* Hillsdale, NJ: The Analytic Press, Inc.

Nathanson, D.L. (1998, August). From empathy to community. Paper presented to the First North American Conference on Conferencing, Minneapolis, MN. http://www.iirp.org/library/ nacc/nacc_nat.html

Nelsen, J. (1996). *Positive Discipline,* 2nd Ed. New York: Ballantine Books.

O'Connell, T. (2002, August). Restorative practices for institutional discipline, complaints and grievance systems. Paper presented at the Third International Conference on Conferencing, Circles and other Restorative Practices, Minneapolis, MN.

Piper, T. (1996). The community standards model: A method to enhance student learning and development. *ACUHO-I Talking Stick,* November, 14-15.

Riestenberg, N. (2002, August). Restorative measures in schools: Evaluation results. Paper presented at the Third International Conference on Conferencing, Circles and other Restorative Practices, Minneapolis, MN.

Satullo, S. (2011). Restorative practices are gaining a foothold in Bethlehem Area School District. Easton, PA: The Express Times, March 6.

Schnell, P. (2002, August). Toward a restorative leadership. Paper presented at the Third International Conference on Conferencing, Circles and other Restorative Practices, Minneapolis, MN.

Simon, B. (1994). *The Empowerment Tradition in American Social Work*. New York: Columbia University Press.

Tomkins, S.S. (1962). *Affect Imagery Consciousness*, Vol. I. New York: Springer.

Tomkins, S.S. (1963). *Affect Imagery Consciousness*, Vol. II. New York: Springer.

Tomkins, S.S. (1987). *Shame*. In D.L. Nathanson (Ed.), *The Many Faces of Shame*. New York: Norton, pp.133-161.

Tomkins, S.S. (1991). *Affect Imagery Consciousness*, Vol. III. New York: Springer.

Tuckman, B. (1965). Developmental sequence in small groups. *Psychological Bulletin* 63 (6): 384-99.

Wachtel, T. (1997). *Real Justice*: Pipersville, PA: The Piper's Press.

Wachtel, T., & McCold, P. (2001). Restorative justice in everyday life. In H. Strang and J. Braithwaite (Eds.), *Restorative Justice and Civil Society*. Cambridge, UK: Cambridge University Press.

Zehr, H. (1990). *Changing Lenses: A New Focus for Crime and Justice*. Scottdale, PA: Herald Press.

Educational Resources

To learn more about DVDs, books and other resources provided by the IIRP, please go to **www.iirp.edu/store**.

DVDs

Burning Bridges

"Burning Bridges" is a 35-minute documentary about the arson of Mood's Bridge, a historic covered bridge in Bucks County, Pennsylvania, USA, and the restorative conference held in its wake. The International Institute for Restorative Practices facilitated this emotional conference, which brought together the six young men who burned down the bridge with their families and members of the community. Using news footage, interviews and video of the actual conference, the documentary tells the story of a community moving through grief and anger to healing.

Four School Conferences: A Composite View

Four actual Real Justice conferences were videotaped, with the permission of participants, at alternative schools operated by the Community Service Foundation and Buxmont Academy, sister nonprofit organizations serving troubled youth in eastern Pennsylvania. Footage from the conferences, which were held for offenses ranging from truancy and leaving school grounds to drug possession and bringing a knife onto a school bus, provide viewers with a realistic view of conferencing. Some conferences are highly emotional; others are not. Some conferences produce satisfying outcomes; others are less successful. But follow-up interviews with conference participants show that even a so-called "unsuccessful" conference can produce meaningful outcomes.

Toxic Talk

"Toxic Talk" shows an actual restorative conference following a workplace incident, in which staff members demeaned their supervisor behind her back and in the presence of customers. The conference, by providing everyone involved with a structured setting to express their emotions freely and honestly, transformed the negative feelings created by the incident into positive ones. The process restored relationships and created a healthier work environment.

DVDs

Facing the Demons

"Facing the Demons" documents the journey of the family and friends of murdered victim Michael Marslew, confronting face-to-face in a conference two of the offenders responsible for Michael's death.

Produced by the Dee Cameron Company, "Facing the Demons" won an award for "best television documentary of 1999" at the 2000 Logies Awards, the Australian equivalent of the Emmy Award, and in 2000 earned the United Nations Association Award for Best Television in its annual Media Peace Awards.

The 30-minute companion DVD "Commentary on Facing the Demons: The Facilitator's Perspective" — which includes commentary by Terry O'Connell, the Australian police sergeant who facilitated the dramatic conference — answers questions and addresses issues raised by the documentary.

A free 8-page study guide is available at:
www.iirp.edu/pdf/FacingTheDemonsStudyGuide.pdf

Conferencing for Serious Offenses:
An Exploration

This thought-provoking, interactive, "do-it-yourself" seminar package provides DVDs (and a CD-ROM with printable Facilitator Guide and Participant Handout) for a group of professionals, students or others to examine the use of restorative conferencing in response to serious offenses.

The seminar package provides detailed directions for using the videos. Also included are instructions on how to run a "circle," which is the format used to structure discussion in the seminar. The use of the circle process provides a truly restorative experience that encourages active participation from everyone attending the seminar.

Please note: *This seminar is not intended to train participants to facilitate restorative conferences, but to enhance their understanding of the potential and the implications of conferencing for serious offenses.*

Visit **www.iirp.edu/store**

Books

The Restorative Practices Handbook for Teachers, Disciplinarians and Administrators

"The Restorative Practices Handbook" is a practical guide for educators interested in implementing restorative practices, an approach that proactively builds positive school communities while dramatically reducing discipline referrals, suspensions and expulsions. The handbook discusses the spectrum of restorative techniques, offers implementation guidelines, explains how and why the processes work, and relates real-world stories of restorative practices in action..

Safer Saner Schools: Restorative Practices in Education

This collection of articles from the Restorative Practices eForum—the IIRP's internet publication with thousands of subscribers around the world—conveys the power of restorative practices to transform schools into positive, vibrant communities while dramatically reducing discipline referrals, detentions and suspensions. The articles include accounts of personal experiences, implementation and research in schools in the United States, Canada, the United Kingdom, Europe, Australia and Asia.

Other Resources

Restorative Questions Poster

This 18" x 24" poster, designed for use in classrooms, prominently displays the essential restorative questions for easy reference in the event of a conflict or harmful incident. The top has questions used to respond to challenging behavior; the bottom has questions to help those harmed by others' actions.

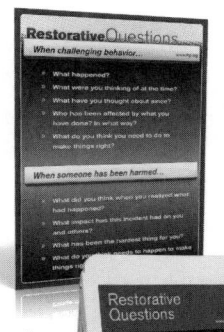

Restorative Questions Sign

This rugged, portable 20" x 35" A-frame sign is designed for use in schools and on playgrounds. It prominently displays the essential restorative questions for easy reference in the event of a conflict or harmful incident. One side has questions used to respond to challenging behavior; the other has questions to help those harmed by others' actions.

Restorative Questions Cards

This pack of 100 handy two-sided coated 2" x 3.5" cards puts the essential restorative questions at your fingertips. One side has questions used to respond to challenging behavior; the other has questions to help those harmed by others' actions. The cards fit easily in a wallet.

IIRP Globe Ball

This small, squeezable globe ball is perfect for use as a talking piece in restorative circles.

Visit **www.iirp.edu/store**

Join the IIRP's Restorative Practices eForum

Be part of a worldwide network of people who are interested in restorative practices. Receive hopeful, useful news about restorative practices efforts in education, criminal justice, family and social services and the workplace.

The Restorative Practices eForum is a free email information service provided by the IIRP. The eForum provides members with occasional short emails that include brief summaries of significant articles, research reports or information about upcoming restorative practices events—with links to full articles.

eForum emails do not include attachments. We do not share our eForum database, so you will receive no spam.

Sign up and view past articles—many of which contain more detailed information about processes described in this book—at **www.iirp.edu/eforum**.

About the IIRP

This volume is a publication of the International Institute for Restorative Practices (IIRP), the world's first graduate school wholly dedicated to the emerging field of restorative practices. The IIRP is engaged in the advanced education of professionals at the graduate level and to the conduct of research that can develop the growing field of restorative practices, with the goal of positively influencing human behavior and strengthening civil society.

The Graduate School offers low-residency master's degree and certificate programs through a mix of traditional, online and hybrid graduate courses and professional development events held around the world. Students may complete a graduate program with little or no travel required to the IIRP campus in Bethlehem, Pennsylvania.

As the world's leading provider of restorative practices education, the IIRP has delivered professional development for tens of thousands of individuals from more than 55 countries working in education, criminal justice and social and human services. To learn more about the IIRP Graduate School, go to **www.iirp.edu**.

About the Authors

Joshua Wachtel is the son of IIRP founding president Ted Wachtel and Community Service Foundation and Buxmont Academy (CSF Buxmont) co-founder Susan Wachtel. He attended a CSF Buxmont alternative school as a senior in high school and taught history and music at CSF Buxmont for four years. He currently resides in western Massachusetts and contributes regularly to the Restorative Practices eForum.

Ted Wachtel is the president and founder of the IIRP. In 1977, Wachtel and his wife, Susan, founded the Community Service Foundation and Buxmont Academy, which operate schools, foster group homes and other programs in Pennsylvania employing restorative practices with delinquent and at-risk youth. Wachtel's publications include *Toughlove,* the best-selling book for parents of troubled adolescents, *Real Justice* and *The Conferencing Handbook,* about restorative conferencing, as well as numerous book chapters and journal articles. He has been a guest speaker at conferences on restorative practices around the world.

Stacey Miller serves as the director of residential life at the University of Vermont where she has worked since 2003. She has over 17 years of progressive professional experience in the area of residential life and housing and has built a solid reputation as an innovative leader in the area of residential community development. Her department's newest initiative is the actualization of the community standards process through the use of restorative practices.